S.C.O.R.E.
for Life

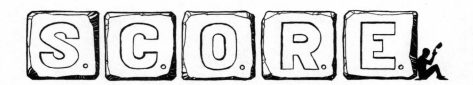

S.C.O.R.E.®
for Life

*The Secret Formula
for Thinking Like a Champion*

JIM FANNIN

Collins

An Imprint of HarperCollinsPublishers

HarperCollins books may be purchased for educational, business, or sales promotional use. For information, please write to: Special Markets Department, HarperCollins Publishers, 10 East 53rd Street, New York, New York 10022.

Designed by Jaime Putorti

Illustrations by Mike Penick, copyright Jim Fannin
S.C.O.R.E.® is a registered trademark of S.C.O.R.E. Performance Systems, Inc.
ZoneCoach® is a registered trademark of Score Performance Systems, Inc.

Library of Congress Cataloging-In-Publication has been applied for.

ISBN-10: 0-06-082325-9
ISBN-13: 978-0-06-082325-2

05   06   07   08   09   10   9   8   7   6   5   4   3   2   1

Contents

Foreword
by Alex Rodriguez

I met Jim Fannin at the very beginning of my professional baseball career. Our meeting was arranged by my Seattle Mariner's teammate Joey Cora. I had marveled at Cora's newfound self-discipline and focus. And I wanted some of that. During my introduction to Jim he asked me what I wanted out of baseball. Quickly I replied, "Hall of Fame." That's a dream every aspiring baseball player has had. He said, "What will you pay?" I thought he was talking about his fee but he said, "My fee is chump change to what you'll make. You'll be able to pay me from your front pocket. I mean . . . what will you sacrifice?" I didn't understand. He told me I'd miss my daughter's birthday or a school play or two. I laughed because I had no children. He said I'd go days without seeing my wife. Of course at this time I didn't even have a serious girlfriend. He replied, "Your journey will have many ups and downs and you'll have to sacrifice your thoughts from friends, family, and other life's indulgences to reach your dream. All great things worthwhile have a price tag of sacrifice."

Over a decade later I have an awesome wife and a beautiful daughter. And Jim was right. I have sacrificed. I do miss my family when I'm on the road. But with the gift of his S.C.O.R.E. System I've learned to manage my thoughts and keep everything simple and balanced.

Jim Fannin has been tough, blunt as a hammer to the head, truthful, relentless, cocky but not arrogant, understanding, reliable, always well dressed, and 99 percent right in the advice he's given. He's been my sounding board, guide, advisor, mentor, therapist, baseball strategist, life coach, and Zone coach. And friend. He's the same now as he was when we first met. Except now he's thinner and in better physical shape. Jim has either left me a phone message or spoken to me in person or on the phone for every game of my career. *Every game*. His attitude has never wavered. I've never heard him talk in a negative way. Ever. He has been an all-night supermarket of encouragement with his 24/7 accessibility. He reminds me of the essence of my craft of baseball every day. For more than 2,000 times he has said to me the following statement . . . "I hit solid with an accelerated bat head." And I've repeated to myself the same mantra at least 10,000 times over the years.

Through the S.C.O.R.E. System I've learned the fine art of visualization and have harnessed the skill of positive self-awareness. I continue to learn to listen to my intuition and act on it immediately. This is my biggest challenge. I apply S.C.O.R.E. to my family, friends, businesses, baseball, and myself. I am constantly learning to think 24/7 like a true champion.

S.C.O.R.E. has many attributes. With it I feel I'm the best prepared I can be. It has helped me adjust during my performances. Life and baseball are about responding to changing conditions and circumstances. I'm making adjustments between pitches and I'm making adjustments at home with my family. This ability has been my biggest asset of late. Jim and the System have also helped me balance my performances. I bounce back quickly after small failures and don't get cocky when I'm awesome. In fact, Jim was with me in Detroit on June 5, 1997, when I became the fifth-youngest player ever to hit for the cycle (home run, triple, double, and single in one game). Immediately after the game he said, "You're only as great as the day after greatness. Next." He has said that exact line after every one of my best games. This balance keeps me grounded.

I never wanted this book written. Now I realize how selfish that was. It amazes me that Jim and S.C.O.R.E. have remained a secret for over thirty years. His clients just didn't want to talk about it. Now after so many years I realize S.C.O.R.E. is something I want my daughter to learn. I see S.C.O.R.E. in the public school system. I envision it taught to the disadvantaged and the unfortunate. With S.C.O.R.E., mindsets can change more easily. It could be used to fight the war on poverty. And with S.C.O.R.E. I see religious, cultural, and ethnic differences not lead to hatred and violence.

So enjoy Jim's life work. I have. Get in the Zone. And if there are any pitchers reading this. . . . I hit solid!

—Alex Rodriguez
8-Time MLB All-Star

Prologue

Have you ever choked during a performance? Have you ever been told how much talent you have, and yet you're not using it? Do you get nervous before a competitive interaction or business transaction? Are you self-conscious or doubtful during performances? Does your level of concentration fluctuate wildly? Do you feel overwhelmed at times?

I'm not ashamed to say I've experienced each and every one of these things.

I've doubled-faulted on match point. I've frozen before speaking to a live audience. I've been intimidated before potential clients. I've repeated the same mistakes over and over due to poor evaluation. I've been confused as a student in the classroom. I've been unprepared before an important performance. I've failed to make adjustments. I've been overwhelmed while juggling too many tasks.

After three decades of studying human performance, I realized these things were normal . . . even for some champions. I had more in common with them than I realized. The champions told me their own performance horror stories. However, they experienced the positive side of a less-than-perfect performance with more regularity than everyone else. And they reached high daily standards, a minimum requirement for a satisfactory performance.

They also frequently experienced the Zone, the state of mind and body where peak performance resides.

The Zone is the moment you perform with complete detachment

from the possibility of failure. This present-tense performance style sets aflame the physical faculties of your body. Your mind and consequently your body possess full alertness and eagerness for action. In this high-octane state of mind, you are so well focused on attaining your goal that others would call your state "tunnel vision."

But it's more than being single-minded or self-centered. Consistently reaching the Zone is a style of life.

My quest for a Zone formula to control how I used my talents and inherent skills stemmed partly from my failures in performance and my passion for excellence.

Like many youngsters, my dream was to play professional sports. I wanted to be a world champion. Although I have competed professionally, I followed a different path as my vocation. Today I coach. My dream manifested itself into not playing against other world champions but coaching them.

My coaching philosophy was developed under the tutelage of Professor R. W. Ross, an 82-year-old African-American schoolteacher—not someone you'd typically see a 12-year-old white boy palling around with in the Appalachian town of Ashland, Kentucky. Nevertheless, the professor was my tennis coach, life mentor, and good friend.

Professor Ross was the human model for my life work. He lived in the Zone until he died at the ripened age of 96. The "Prof" observed and thought cautiously before speaking. He spoke softly in short, staccato sentences. He wasted no words. Everything about him was efficient, from the way he moved to the way he ate, spoke, and thought. He used silence to trim mental waste with the skill of a surgeon. I was an ambitious student who absorbed the professor's every word.

The foundation for my teaching craft was laid with his skill and acumen. He trained me to motivate five- and six-year-old children in tennis when I was only a kid myself. Imagery, concentration, self-esteem, and self-discipline were new concepts to me that he sprinkled along my journey through adolescence.

The professor fueled my desire to coach and sparked my new-found curiosity regarding maximizing performance. He showed me the ingredients for greatness. Those building blocks later became the foundation of my S.C.O.R.E. Performance System. He taught me that practitioners of the Zone possess positive mental health and spiritual growth in all of life's arenas. He introduced me to the power of visualization and the tools of self-awareness.

With the wisdom from the professor and my relentless pursuit of excellence, I was awarded a college scholarship in tennis to East Tennessee State University. Here I fought my way to an Ohio Valley Conference tennis championship. My parents and the professor were so proud. With a degree under my arm, I used the three Rs to get a job. In Kentucky terms, those were readin', ritin', and Route 23 — the road north to the big cities. Here I landed a job at the Columbus Indoor Tennis Club in Columbus, Ohio, and my formal career began.

I took a leave of absence from work to play professional tennis tournaments on the slow red-clay courts of Europe. I lost in every country but Belgium. I've never been to Belgium. I returned to the States with my career path more narrow.

Now in my early twenties, I had the privilege of interviewing scores of champions from all walks of life on why they were so successful. From CEO Charles Y. Lazarus (of Federated Department Stores), Ohio governor John Gilligan, Howard Sirak (heart surgeon), Barry Zacks (founder of Max & Irma's restaurant chain), Dick Kitch (tennis professional), George Skestos (real-estate developer), Ben Zox and Paul Scott (successful attorneys), and Millard Cummins (entrepreneur) to Jimmy Connors (former world's number one male tennis player), Chris Evert (former world's number one female tennis player), and Arthur Ashe (tennis great, author, and humanitarian), I picked their minds for answers to this question: what makes you great? I brought my findings to my next life coach . . . my father. I told him that the formula for Zone attainment was getting confusing. I understood all of the ingredients, but I was unsure how it worked in a simple recipe. James Edward Fannin, my father, was an uneducated word-smith. My dad could finish the *New York Times* crossword puzzle in one sitting. "How did you know the sun god's name is Ra?" I asked. He replied, "You didn't learn that in college?"

Here is how S.C.O.R.E. came about.

My father took Webster's dictionary and wrote every intangible word on a three-by-five index card. Love, honestly, discipline, focus, confidence, passion, and hundreds of other words were strewn across his living-room floor. When I walked into his home, I said, "What is this mess?" He replied, "Inside this room is the answer to your question of how to get into the Zone. What did the champions tell you first about their success?" I said, "They all had a vision or dream and they illuminated a pathway to attain it." He said, "That's self-discipline. Let's place it first." And with that we arranged other words that fit under the heading of self-discipline. Those were vision, patience, goals, tasks, persistence, and so. "What's next?" he queried. I said, "They all had the ability to focus with blinders." With that statement my father placed the concentration index card next to self-discipline. I thought, "You can't focus unless you have a place to send your energy." Concentration must come after self-discipline. Next? All champion interviewees had tremendous confidence and high self-esteem. My father said, "We need the word *optimism*. In fact, you have to have optimism, or I can't help anymore." Laughing, I said, "Why?" "Because I'm the president of the Ashland Optimist Club [a men's service club like Kiwanis or Rotary]," he replied. So, reluctantly, I placed the optimism index card next to the concentration card on the floor. We then placed all the other words that fit under that heading. I knew optimism was the glue that held these champions together. What else was next? It's not what they said, but how they went about their profession. They all seemed effortless and smooth in the execution of their craft. So my dad and I placed the relaxation index card next to optimism. "What else did you observe from the champions?" "Dad, they all loved what they did. They had great passion for their craft." And with that he said, "Enjoyment." They all enjoyed what they did. That's the bottom-line end product for every champion.

With most of the index cards in single file under Self-discipline, Concentration, Optimism, Relaxation, and Enjoyment my father blurted out, "It's an acronym! And don't tell me you didn't learn that in college, either." Wow! It was an acronym or a word where its letters represent other words. S.C.O.R.E. was born in 1974. My father's living room floor looked something like the following graphic.

S	C	O	R	E
Goals	Focusing	Confidence	Effortless	Enthusiasm
Tolerance	Channeling	Self-Esteem	Calm	Excitement
Patience	Accuracy	Determined	Peace	Desire
Direction	Productive	Faith	Smooth	Energy
Control	Intense	Hope	Tranquil	Movement
Strategy	Detail	Belief	Serene	Happy
Tactics	Tasks	Positive	Harmony	Fun
Persevere	Laserlike	Expectancy	Ease	Eager
Simplicity	Efficiency	Trust	Comfort	Passion
Targets	Center	Possible	Fluid	Vitality

Soon I incorporated S.C.O.R.E. into a new tennis teaching system for children between the ages of four and eight called Tennis Tots. The instructors were trained in the S.C.O.R.E. System. Maximize the S.C.O.R.E. Level of the students and learning would be maximized. The program swiftly became successful. With the aid of a self-financed research project with three Ohio State University professors, I decided to add new information to my teaching. How to facilitate super learning was my quest. I found that we learned more from birth to five years old than the rest of our lives combined. I also learned that we naturally possess the formula for success in our most formative age. Then most of us lose the formula, although we will see how some champions gain it back.

After this research, I franchised my Tennis Tots program and sold 43 of them throughout the Midwest and Colorado with seven licenses sold in Great Britain. By observing and teaching hundreds of teachers worldwide, we reached over 100,000 children with the S.C.O.R.E. System.

I wrote my first book about S.C.O.R.E., called *Tennis & Kids: The Family Connection* (Doubleday, 1979). Hundreds of parent seminars followed. During the seminars, I was asked, "Does S.C.O.R.E. work for baseball?" Yes. "Does S.C.O.R.E. work for golf?" Yes. "Can you come speak to my company?" Yes. Because most of my Tennis Tots franchises were located in Chicago, I moved there permanently. It has been my home since 1978.

I was also coaching the best tennis players in the world. At one time I was training eight pros in the world's top 60. It was here that I became proficient at ascertaining exactly what my clients needed to do to reverse a poor performance. And I gave them S.C.O.R.E. signals from the stands during every match. Within seconds, they took my cues and altered their matches. They responded with seven players reaching the world's top 10 ranking.

In 1983, I purchased a 60,000-square-foot sports center in the Chicago suburbs. Here I founded the S.C.O.R.E. Tennis Academy, where hundreds of juniors trained. By the time we sold the club in 1999, we had housed eight national champions, two Illinois high-school champions, four Illinois high-school team champions, and over 100 college scholarship recipients (our greatest accomplishment).

I continue to hone my craft of propagating Zone attainment. To date, I've conducted thousands of corporate, parent, and student-athlete seminars and clinics in the S.C.O.R.E. System. One hundred professional athletes have taken S.C.O.R.E. into battle in eight different sports. Nineteen Major League Baseball all-stars have used the

System to give them an edge over the competition. Five PGA Tour players won their first tournament with S.C.O.R.E. in their golf bag. Corporations have earned millions of dollars by changing how they think with S.C.O.R.E.

From center court at Wimbledon to the gridiron of the Super Bowl to the diamonds of the World Series to the hardwood floors of the NBA play-offs to the fairways of the Masters, the S.C.O.R.E. System has been there. More important, I've dedicated my time and energy in developing the S.C.O.R.E. System into a simple day-to-day performance formula useful for everyone.

The S.C.O.R.E. System is based on the following principles.

- You possess free will.
- Only you possess your thoughts.
- No thoughts can enter your mind as your own without your permission.
- You cannot hold a positive and negative thought simultaneously in your mind.
- You can prepare your subconscious mind (the performance automatic pilot) for positive results.
- Your thoughts dictate your physical actions.
- Your collection of thoughts and the corresponding verbal and nonverbal reactions to these thoughts determine your attitude.
- This attitude consists of a domino-like chain of intangibles that form an acronym called S.C.O.R.E. The acronym represents Self-discipline, Concentration, Optimism, Relaxation, and Enjoyment.
- S.C.O.R.E. comes with its own language that *can* and *will* be used to communicate with you, family members, relationships, coaches, teammates, clients, and prospective clients, and can be used against the opposition.
- Everyone possesses a high or low level of S.C.O.R.E. at any given time.

- Changes in your S.C.O.R.E. and the competition's S.C.O.R.E. is an absolute.
- There are three time elements to every performance: pre-performance, performance, and post-performance.
- Managing S.C.O.R.E. as you pass through the three performance time segments is the key to peak performance.

I have never once seen S.C.O.R.E. fail its students, though I have witnessed the reverse countless times. It is not a panacea for winning every performance, but it is a tried and proven blueprint for potential realization, the art of a real winner. Once you embrace this recipe for success, you'll immediately see positive change. Commitment and a consistent use of this success formula will enable you to see a clear path to personal or professional achievement. You will find as you learn more about the System and about yourself that you may alter the prescription dosage of S.C.O.R.E. according to your own personality, situation, and mission.

As you embark on this venture, please remember the importance of commitment. It is essential you embrace the mission, philosophy, principles, strategy, and tactics of the S.C.O.R.E. System. Without this commitment, the information contained in this book can merely assist your performances, rather than catapult you to peak performance.

For 30 years now, I have trained elite performers. I coach champions, using techniques gleaned from research and experience. But the Zone has benefited me as well: I've traveled the world, made a great living, and had a blast. I am a husband, a father, and a good friend. Three decades of performing in the Zone has been an awesome experience.

My parents set me on the right track early. As an only child, I was raised with love and devotion to my well-being. Even though we started out poor in the Appalachian hills of eastern Kentucky, I was never allowed to be aware of it.

When my father died, he left a void. He was a mentor and guide. I still feel his loss. When my mother became sick several years ago, I was at her bedside like she had been at mine in my formative years. I could not imagine losing her as she rapidly neared the end of her life. She was my biggest fan and reveled in the considerable success I had achieved. But, while my only thoughts were for her well-being, she still was thinking of the potential she saw in me that remained untapped, areas I had been too timid to broach. Minutes before she passed away, she looked me in the eye and said, "Go for it." As I urged her to relax and breathe, she repeated it: "S.C.O.R.E. Go for it." She died minutes later in my arms. I was devastated, but took solace in the promise I had made to her: "I will, Mom." At the age of 55, I am writing this book and keeping my promise.

I enjoy my life's work. Although it took me over 30 years to provide this information, you'll be applying it successfully within just a few hours. Godspeed, and remember: "Good fortune favors the bold!"

Jim Fannin
ZoneCoach

S.C.O.R.E.
for Life

CHAPTER 1

The Mind of a Champion

Since you picked up this book, I can predict the following: you want more than you have now—more success, more wealth, more love, and more happiness. We all see images of successful people. We all dream of the perfect job, achieving new wealth, of living the life we choose in harmony with the people we love. For many of us, the dream stops there. We wonder what leads some extraordinary people to confront and exceed their goals and compete at the highest level, while others of us run in place, distracted and intimidated by our fears—even as we work harder and harder, and study various programs for personal fulfillment.

In this book, I will share with you a collection of ideas and daily exercises that transform everyday performers into true champions. This system has made me one of the leading experts in human potential, and catapulted business leaders and athletes from the middle of the pack to the greatest in their game. This program starts with a question: Would you invest just three hours a week spread out in bursts of 30, 60, or 90 seconds over a seven-day period to become a champion? This I know from three decades of coaching: by using the S.C.O.R.E. Performance System, you will build the habits that will make you a champion. Throughout this book I will use the pronouns *he, she, him, her,* and so on interchangeably. I want to make it clear that true champions have no specific gender, age, or experience. When I use the words *he* and *him,* ladies, please realize I'm still speaking directly to you. And gentlemen, the same goes for you. I coach champions, not gender, race, age, affiliation, or experience. Period!

There are three types of people: nonchampions, champions, and true champions.

Every day as we go to work or school we pass a multitude of nonchampions. Most of these people have champion moments, days, or even weeks. But too often, they are sidetracked with many interruptions and distractions. Too often, we lose the mind-set of a champion. The energy and passion we feel when we are locked in the moment is lost. We wake up in the morning unsure of our own vision for our lives. Rather than attack the day with positive thoughts and actions, we think and speak in negatives, or criticize others without an awareness of the damaging effects of our language on our family, colleagues, or friends. We gossip. We worry. We envy. We procrastinate. Even as we admonish ourselves for dissipating our energies this way, we fall into the habits that ground us in mediocrity and a stale feeling of dissatisfaction. Through three decades of coaching athletes and professionals, and studying the best science about human performance, I've found three markers of mediocre, nonchampion living that defeat our best intentions:

- We think too much, rehashing the past and projecting negativity into the future.
- We talk too much, mostly about things that don't matter.
- We produce too little; and when we go home at night and lay our heads on our pillow, we feel our day just didn't have enough time.

The result? Nonchampions live on a roller coaster of thought and emotion. We are disciplined in one moment and undisciplined the next. Our concentration fluctuates. We are not confident in how we look and are pessimistic in what we can achieve. We are stressed to the max, and we put on masks to hide our painful sense of inadequacy. As often as we mislead others, we mislead ourselves. We may touch the Zone on our best days, but we do not live in the Zone.

A *champion* prepares to win before they enter the arena. A champion manages the five intangibles of *Self-Discipline, Concentration, Optimism, Relaxation,* and *Enjoyment* on a daily basis. Before a champion goes to work, she is ready for the day to unfold successfully. She has a plan and the strategy and tactics to support the plan. A champion is armed with mental tools he can wield with swiftness and accuracy to adjust to changing conditions and circumstances. A champion is prepared to handle the surprise arrival of adversity.

The champion is honest. She tells it like it is. She evaluates her performance objectively on a continuous basis. Regardless of the outcome, she remains confident in her abilities. She learns from her mistakes. She improves every day.

A champion thinks less and produces more. Her pathway to success is illuminated. She sees it clearly. When a champion goes off course, he recovers swiftly. Success is getting up one more time from defeat. By thinking differently, he thinks like a champion.

We see, hear, and read about champions every day on television, the radio, and the Internet, or in magazines and newspapers: the Olympian who trains his or her entire life and finally wins the gold medal; the baseball player who makes the game-winning hit to win the World Series; the actor or actress who gives an acceptance speech at the Oscars; the tennis star who serves an ace to win Wimbledon; the business person who closes that multimillion-dollar deal. These people seem to have it all—a successful career, a big house on the hill, a fancy car, and 2.5 kids. Champions? By most people's definition, yes. The dictionary defines a *chăm'-pē-an* as one who wins first place or first prize in a competition or one who is clearly superior or has the attributes of a winner. By this definition, these people are champions.

I've known many individuals who became champions in baseball, golf, banking, or sales but faced major struggles in life's other arenas, from divorce to partnership squabbles to poor health to parenting issues. In this book, I challenge you as I have challenged all of my most successful clients, to reach an even higher goal: to go beyond performing like a champion to living the life of a *true champion*.

What makes a true champion? The true champion is very rare. She stands out in a crowd. She is energized. You can feel her presence. What is the difference in a champion and a true champion? A true champion has no time off. Living in the Zone is a full-time job.

A *true champion* is a champion on and off the field and in and out of the office. Being a true champion is a full-time job.

A true champion is not just a champion in a sport or a champion at work. This person is a champion in every one of her life arenas.

When a champion reaches the top, he stays at the top. He thrives at the top. Most of all, a true champion is energized and carried by a state of mind that seeks balance and simplicity. A true champion on the field is just as big a champion off the field. His tireless pursuit of being the best he can be is apparent in his health and wellness, at work, in his hobbies, at home, and with his family and friends. Even among perfect strangers, he uplifts and inspires others. Are you a true champion?

True champions can be everyday people, like the firefighter who goes up the stairs of a burning building while everyone else is running out, and then returns home to the role of great spouse and awesome father, without missing a beat. True champions include the salesperson who goes above the call of duty to help his company succeed — and goes beyond the call of duty in his personal life with family and friends. True champions include the mom who diligently teaches her kids values and morals while juggling multiple schedules like an air-traffic controller. True champions are successful at whatever they do. They cut through all the chaos in their lives. They are effortless, disciplined, patient, poised, and *focused*. You can feel their energy as they move into the room — confident, with their heads held high, their postures erect. They have a presence about them just in the way they carry themselves. You look at them and feel, "They know — they get it!" And they make everybody else better — everybody on the team.

The best thing about living as a true champion is that it's fun. Even when the pressure is intense, even during that moment of truth when you know the next move this person makes is going to decide whether they win or lose, true champions have a passion and an enthusiasm that's so exciting to watch. That's why we do watch: because we want to be like that.

So from now on, when I refer to being a champion, keep in mind the true champion who knows the S.C.O.R.E. And after reading this book, the true champion that I'm speaking of will be *you!*

Throughout this book, you will find a number of exercises to complete. I recommend highly that you participate in each and every one along the way. There are no shortcuts to becoming a true champion. These exercises are designed to stimulate your mind and activate your body to begin to think and act differently, like a world champion. So here we go.

CHAMPIONS YOU ADMIRE

Take a blank piece of paper. On the top of the paper, write the names of five people who you see as champions. These people do not have to be rich or famous, but anyone whom you feel exudes the qualities of a champion. Below each name write down five one- or two-word qualities of the person. For example, describe your mother: passionate, soft-spoken, loving, dedicated, and energetic. Or describe Michael Jordan: focused, confident, effortless, competitive, and passionate. What champion qualities are written more than once? Do you exude these qualities? Take possession of them. Make them your own.

No matter your ethnic background, or where you come from or what you do for a living, we all want the same things in life. We want a successful career doing something that we love to do. We want to be loved by someone special. We want to have a happy and healthy family. We want to enjoy life. These desires are universal. So why do so many people work at jobs they can't stand, have trouble falling in love, constantly fight with their family members, and struggle with their own health and wellness? Because they don't *think like a champion.*

How many times do we see someone go to the top of their profession and then seemingly overnight they fall from grace? A true champion has the ability to stay a champion. So why do true champions consistently succeed? *Champions think differently.* They have mastered the art of balance and simplicity in their lives. But before I get into the science behind this, I want you to experience your second exercise.

DO YOU THINK LIKE A CHAMPION?

This is a short quiz to see how your thoughts measure up against the best championship minds. There are only two possible answers: Yes or No. Answer them honestly. Don't worry about right or wrong answers. Don't worry if you get a low score. You will take an in-depth test at the end of this book. What you will read and learn in this book will change your thoughts and belief system. Your score will be higher on the final test.

YES *or* NO

1. *I have a vision for my life.* __Y__
2. *I separate my life into different areas or arenas.* __Y__
3. *I have a vision for each area of my life.* _____
4. *I am prepared before my performances.* __Y__
5. *I have marked and measurable goals in my life.* __Y__
6. *I evaluate objectively all of my performances.* __Y__
7. *I make positive adjustments in tough situations.* __Y__
8. *When I come home to my family, I leave my work at the office.* __N__
9. *I can focus for a long period of time when I'm working.* __N__
10. *I am not easily distracted during a performance.* __Y__
11. *I visualize my goals regularly.* __Y__
12. *I perform in the present tense.* _____
13. *I have supreme confidence in everything I do.* __N__
14. *I win in my mind before I compete.* __Y__
15. *I am calm and comfortable with adversity.* __Y__
16. *I make people comfortable and relaxed when I'm around.* __Y__
17. *I perform without worry or anxiety.* __N__
18. *I make people smile.* __Y__
19. *I perform at my own rhythm and tempo.* __Y__
20. *I am totally happy with what I do for a living.* __Y__

21. *I show high enthusiasm before, during, and after my perform-ances.* ____
22. *I love to perform in competitive situations.* ____
23. *I enjoy solving problems.* ____
24. *I lead by example.* ____
25. *I seldom think about the past.* ____

If you have answered NO to three or more of these statements, you DO NOT think like a champion. If you answered YES to all of them, you are there. If so, use this book as a refresher course to keep you on track. One of the keys of becoming a champion is staying a champion. Remember to take the final exam at the conclusion of the book.

Thoughts can last just a few seconds to over a minute, with the average thought lasting 14 seconds, according to Dr. Eric Klinger of the University of Minnesota, Morris. Our thoughts can focus on the future, the past, or the now. They can be positive or negative. However, we cannot have a positive thought and a negative thought simultaneously. Our thoughts are either focused or scattered. The average person has between 2,000 and 3,000 thoughts per day with 60 percent of these thoughts in mental chaos. During an out-of-control day, our brain can entertain even more thoughts, shattering our focus and sense of self-control. To understand the thought discipline of a true champion, let's turn to a surprising model: babies. I'll explain.

From the time you were born until approximately the age of five, you learned more in those 60 months than you will learn in the rest of your life. When you were born, you had very few thoughts: "I need some food." "I want my Mom." "I need to sleep." Or, "Hey I pooped my pants—I'm uncomfortable." Simple and focused. You had no thoughts of what happened yesterday or what might happen tomorrow. Your only thought was about the now.

As the months of your life rolled on, you began to formalize more complex thoughts—but the vast majority of your thoughts were still centered on the moment. You were engaged in your environment. You had no concept of time. You never thought of the past or the future. You saw everything. You questioned everything. Why became a common word. You told the truth. As an overweight stranger walked by, you'd say, "Why are you so fat?" Or you'd say: "Why is your skin black?" "Why are your teeth crooked?" "Why is the sky blue?"

Poor mom and dad—your imagination was vivid and wild. With one thought, you could be a cowboy, a space traveler, a ballerina, or a baseball player in just a matter of seconds. If you were hungry, you let everyone know it. Immediately! If you were tired, you laid down, anywhere—even if it was in the middle of a store.

But something begins to happen when we reach age six. We start getting bombarded with chaotic information. More and more, adults introduce the sense of the future and the past. The future: "Are you going to be a big boy someday?" "Someday you'll grow up to be a doctor." And the past: "How many times have I told you not to do that!" Your belief system started to change: "You'll never have a boyfriend if you keep acting like that." "What's wrong with you?" The following example highlights this point.

I've coached some of the best athletes and business executives in the world but teaching kids has always been my passion. In 1971, I created a program called Tennis Tots, which quickly had an enrollment of more than one thousand students. The program was getting serious, and I was determined to make it the best in the country before I would franchise it. So I hired three PhDs from Ohio State University to assist me in creating a program for maximizing learning.

With the gymnasium full of five-year-old children, the group was told the following: "If you're fast, real fast, go over to this side of the gym. If you're slow, not fast, go to the other side of the gym." No one moved. There were two boys in the front of the group, Billy and Brent. Billy was the largest child in the group. He looked slow. Brent was small and wiry. He looked fast. Brent nudged Billy and said, "Go on Billy. You know you're slow. Go to the slow side." At the cruel bluntness of Brent's words, Billy's shoulders slumped, and he proceeded to lumber over to the slow side. Brent sprinted to the fast side with a smile on his face. The rest of the group did not divide evenly. In fact, we had to put pressure on some students, demanding that they show us how they perceived their speed of foot.

Next, we tested each child's speed while running the 40-yard dash. Every time was recorded without any child knowing his marks. Astonishingly, some of the "slow" kids actually ran faster than the supposedly fleeter kids. The group was reassembled into the original groups of fast and slow kids. Then we announced that the slow kids wanted to race the fast kids. The slow kids looked stunned. We then paired up one-on-one races between the "fast" and "slow" kids. Many of the "slower" kids were actually faster than the "faster" kid that they were paired with.

The child who thought he was slow but in fact ran the fastest sprinted into the lead 98 percent of the time. But then the kids' mental hardwiring took over, and with only 10 yards to go in the race, the same kid that thought he or she was slow actually slowed down and lost the race, holding true to their belief and expectations. This occurred 92 percent of the time.

When I was 12 years old, I befriended an 82-year-old retired schoolteacher named Professor R. W. Ross. He directed the YMCA tennis program. He became my mentor, and I became his assistant in coaching the younger kids. When he spoke, he commanded your full attention. He told me: "Change how a person thinks, and you will change how they feel. Change how they feel, and you will change how they perform. Change how they perform and you'll change results. Change results, and you'll change their lives."

Over the next few weeks, we changed the way the "slow" kids thought. We helped them believe they were fast. By changing their belief system from slow to fast, they reversed their losses. I'm sure there are some whose life changed that day.

With this new information tucked under my arm, I began to approach the world with a totally different outlook. For 30 years, I studied with great interest how the champion's mind worked, spurring my curiosity about peak performance. It was in the late 1970s and early 1980s that I began interviewing world champions from different sports and industries. I always thought that champions did something extraordinarily special. You know what? They do. After coaching 50 professional athletes and talking to dozens of corporate CEOs, I began to put it together. The true champion does very little unnecessary thinking. The world champion doesn't have 2,000 to 3,000 thoughts per day. *The world champion has approximately 1,100 to 1,300 thoughts per day.*

True champions think less but hold a thought for a longer period of time. The first fundamental of becoming a true champion is learning how to think *less*, not more. That is the *real* challenge. True champions turn the old adage "Less is more" into "Fewer thoughts produce more results."

How ironic! The world champion has approximately the same number of thoughts as a young child. Both the champion and the child have many things in common. They possess no worries. They do not gossip or spread rumors. They are honest with themselves. They have great imaginations. They spend the majority of their time in the moment. They leave the past in the past and do not return. "That's hot. I won't touch that again," thinks the child. "This pitcher throws fast. I'll quicken my bat speed," thinks the champion. They perform detached from the future. By disengaging, the champion performs effortlessly without anxiety of the pending outcome. The child performs with that same freedom. Both the champion and the child perform in the mind-set called the Zone.

Helping people achieve the Zone is my passion, my life's work, and my vocation. I am the Zone Coach. And you are now my peak performer. It's time to learn how you perform like a champion in the Zone.

CHAPTER 2

The Power of the Zone

When you get into the Zone, you have harnessed the power of the ultimate fusion of mind and body. Corporations and athletes from around the world have spent billions of dollars seeking this state of being. I receive phone calls every single day from professional athletes and executives who want to learn more about attracting this frame of mind that ignites the body to peak performance. You've witnessed great performers in the Zone:

- Lance Armstrong winning the Tour de France
- Michael Jordan soaring in the NBA Finals
- Tiger Woods dominating the PGA Tour in 2000

- The U.S. hockey team defeating the Russians to win the gold medal in 1980
- Rudy Giuliani managing the crisis in New York during the 9/11 terrorist attacks

The Zone is literally your fight or flight response to stress or trauma. Stress attracts the Zone. There are two types of stress. First is the stress that we don't want. This results from an accident, threatening situation, or life-altering experience. It could also occur from an overbearing boss, financial pressure, or the tension of a failed relationship. Then there is stress that you place on yourself on your own terms and conditions. This stress is good. It is the best friend of the champion. But it is *not* the type of stress that you might think. Different levels of this good stress produce different levels of the Zone.

As children, our innate drive to learn creates a level of positive stress that accelerates our learning. The great newspaper reporter uses stress from impending deadlines to write award-winning stories. Leading sales executives use stress from meeting monthly and year-end quotas to catapult them over the competition. In these cases, stress is good.

The traumatic stress from an impending danger in fact creates a state that I know to be the Zone. Here the Zone acts as a mental airbag to protect you or others from harm's way. In a life-or-death situation, the Zone raises you to the performance level that gives you the best chance of emerging victorious from the prospects of defeat.

Here is an extreme example.

You're standing outside, across the street from a building. You look and see a young boy crying and screaming from a window. The building is on fire. Flames are shooting out of the roof. You know in that moment that something must be done to save this child.

Your conscious mind immediately shuts down. Your intuition, powered by your subconscious mind, takes over. The brain's autopilot adjusts your body for the task at hand. A chemical cocktail is fuel-injected into your blood stream for high-octane energy. In an instant, your heart rate quickens. Your skin sensitivity is heightened. Your eyes double or triple shutter speed to give you the illusion that everything is in slow motion—that's so you can more easily find avenues of rescue and escape.

Without thoughts of consequence, you rush into the building. You are detached from the impending danger. Your stomach has already shut down. The digestive process has abruptly been interrupted. The stomach diverts blood to your brain so that you have clarity, and to the large muscles so that you have inordinate speed, strength, balance, and agility. The smoke is everywhere. You can't see a foot in front of you, but an intuitive force is now taking over. It's guiding you from room to room while you listen for the voice of the crying child. Sure enough, you find him.

As you run out of the building with the child in your arms, the event seems surreal. It's as if it was happening to another person or like it was a dream. People gather around you. Someone calls you a hero. You just think, "Anyone would have done that. I didn't do anything special."

Within minutes of the ordeal, the blood flows back to your stomach. You might get nauseous or even throw up. Fear creeps back into your mind. You might even start to cry. Then and only then do you realize what happened.

But for the moment that you were in the building, the fight-or-flight syndrome from traumatic stress put you into a Zone state of mind: this is where heroes go. This is the place of the champion.

Do you have to have traumatic stress to get in the Zone?

To be sure, life-threatening events are far from the only pathways to the Zone. Each of us was born with the secret formula to attract the

Zone. This formula was buried in the DNA that was passed from your parents to you at birth.

You have experienced the Zone many times in your life . . . most likely without ever knowing it. Sometimes it lasted for a minute or for a full performance or even an entire day or week. It is those times in your life when you feel most alive. Things just seem to click. You feel connected. You feel that nothing can go wrong. Your relationships are rewarding. Opportunities appear all around you. The classic "bad day" disappears. A purposeful calm comes over you. The people around you feel your energy. Your intuition is razor sharp. Coincidence is commonplace. And best of all, money flows.

The Zone is a phenomenon that you possess now.

It has many synonyms. Clickin', raking, vibing, playing out of my mind, on all cylinders, in the groove, on fire, treeing, dial-a-pitch, in the flow, and in sync are just a few.

After watching Chicago Bulls great Michael Jordan drop 42 points on the opposition, I was in the locker room after the game discussing his other passion—golf. The Zone was brought up, and he said, "I know the Zone. I can put it on like an overcoat." You saw him play. I believe he could.

The Zone is that state of mind where records are broken, goals are reached, and dreams are realized. It is a state of mind where we feel everything is possible. It is manifested physically, emotionally, and intuitively. You are totally immersed in what you are doing.

EXERCISE #3

THE POWER OF NOW: THE ZONE EXAMPLE

Because the Zone exists only in the now, here is an exercise to show the power of being in the present tense. Take a small object—a small ball would be the best. Toss the object into the air and catch it three times. Make it easy to catch. Do not read any further until you complete this task. Do it, now.

So what happened? Did you catch it? Did you worry about catching it? Did you ponder what would happen after you caught it? NO. You just did it. No thought of the past. No thought of the future. You just performed in the now. You didn't think about when to pick up the kids, or finishing your homework, or the meeting you have at the office tomorrow. You only thought about catching the ball. Nothing more . . . nothing less. That's the power of the now. The Zone is only obtained by being in the now! Champions understand this fact and use it to their advantage. Are you in the now?

I first remember being in the Zone on the playground as a child back in my home state of Kentucky. I played with no thought of time. I had no thoughts of the past or the future. I was engrossed in play with my buddies. My mom had to yell my name over and over just to get me to come home for dinner. I was engaged in the games I played with my friends. I was locked in the NOW.

I was in the Zone. You've experienced similar scenarios as a kid.

I recall pitching a one-hitter in Little League baseball. I was focused on the target inside the catcher's mitt. Time seemed to stand still. I had a feeling of dominance. I did not think of the outcome. I was too busy pitching.

I was in the Zone. You likely experienced this same mind-set when you played in organized sports in junior high, high school, or college — or just felt the exhilaration of achieving a personal best in running, rock climbing, or swimming.

I remember closing the sale on eight houses in a row while working door-to-door for the Fuller Brush Company as a 14-year old salesman. I led Kentucky in sales. I was on a roll. Money flowed. My intuition was razor sharp. I could tell if I was going to make a sale within 90 seconds from my front porch introduction. I was in the

Zone. You've been here during a sales presentation, at a business meeting, or during a speech or a formal gathering.

I scored a perfect 100 on an anatomy test in college. I needed that score to get an A for the semester. I remember seeing the answers in my mind exactly how they appeared on the pages of the book as I took the exam. It was so simple. It seemed easy. I felt extremely smart.

I was in the Zone. I know you have experienced this in high school or college and in many other instances that have happened in your life. You have performed in the Zone many times . . . and you have also been out of the Zone.

Although stressful events associated with trauma are the most common pathways to the Zone, there is a way to deliver the Zone to your life without negative stress. The Zone is volatile. When you are aware of being in it, it is already gone. You can attract and repel it with a single thought. I have developed a systematic way of thinking that has attracted the Zone for hundreds of professional athletes and thousands of executives, coaches, and students. It is called the S.C.O.R.E. Performance System.

The S.C.O.R.E. System helps you think about what you think about.

It helps you understand attitude. Attitude is your collective thought at any given time. When you change your thoughts, you change your attitude. When you change your attitude, you change your actions. When you change your actions, you change your results. When you change results, you change your destiny.

Thoughts can make you a champion by attracting the Zone or they can keep you shackled as a nonchampion by repelling this mind-set.

How powerful is one thought?

One thought is a literal action. It can be measured as an electrical current in your brain. Of course, you know for every action there is a reaction. However, a thought brings three reactions: physical, emotional, and intuitive.

First, each thought has a *physical* reaction. Think something sad and you will look sad. Think something funny and you smile or laugh. A true champion looks like a winner: confident and poised. A non-champion looks defeated and dejected. All because of how you thought. Can you mask the physical reaction to your thoughts? Yes. You can have a poker face, but most of us don't. How many times have you been accused of a "dirty look" that you believe didn't happen? "I didn't give you a dirty look," we proclaim. How many times has someone asked you, "Are you okay? What's wrong?" And you respond with "I'm fine. Why do you ask?" Most of us are readable. Many times we are unaware of our telltale mannerisms. Each of our thoughts have physical reactions in our voice inflection, hand gestures, posture, eye movements, breathing, and overall movements. We must be careful in what we think. We can tip off the alert people around us to our innermost thoughts.

Second, each thought has an *emotional* reaction. Think a sad thought and your serotonin level changes and you feel sad. Think a happy thought and endorphins enter your bloodstream and you feel happy. Can you mask the emotional reactions to your thoughts? Most of us cannot. We leave our emotion on our sleeve for all to see. All of our feelings emanate from a thought. Each thought can trigger a chemical change in our bodies that gives us the feelings of envy, rage, frustration, jealousy, sadness, or despair. If you do not like how you feel, change how you are thinking.

Everyone that sees you today, tomorrow, or next week can see your body language. They can feel your emotion. You are readable. The champion understands this.

Last, your thoughts have an *intuitive* reaction. Each thought sends vibrations from the brain out into the environment. These projected vibes have no geographical boundaries. You are capable of sending and receiving these vibrations with different skill levels. They are re-

ceived as images in the mind—no different than a television signal transmission. Your mother was probably a master at this. She could sense danger for you, even when you were in another room. She could feel that something was wrong, even if you were in another part of the country. "A little bird told me" or "I have eyes in the back of my head," she might have said.

Every thought you have has an intuitive reaction. This cannot be masked. We send and receive vibes. They come in the form of a hunch, a gut feeling, or a sense of knowing.

Remember, the average person has over 2,000 thoughts per day. All of these thoughts have reactions that can be seen and felt by everyone around you: team members, associates, family, friends, and opponents. Your thoughts cause worry, anxiety, envy, jealousy, impatience, frustration, sadness, apathy, or despair.

Have you ever had a *bad* day—the opposite of a Zone performance? You know what I mean—when your mind is in complete chaos and the present, the now, is so elusive that it seems every one of your thoughts lie in the future or the past. You are putting out fires at the office. Murphy's Law prevails. All areas of your life bombard you at once. Your children need your attention. Maybe your spouse, boss, or parents are getting on your nerves. Your best friend, who has unloaded all of his problems at your doorstep, is demanding your time, and there is none to be had. And at the end of the day you are tired, realizing you accomplished nothing on your list of things to do.

Most people know to stay out of your way. Your thoughts are radiating chaos. You are a walking neon sign of negativity.

This is the thinking of a nonchampion. This is *not* being in the Zone. I don't believe in bad days. Neither does the true champion.

I know you don't want to think in a negative way. I know you want to think like a true champion. I know you would like to have fewer thoughts. In fact, you might even want to be a kid again. I know you would like to attract the Zone. You need to know the S.C.O.R.E.

> *Every thought you have has an intuitive reaction. This cannot be masked. We send and receive vibes. They come in the form of a hunch, a gut feeling, or a sense of knowing.*

Here's where the S.C.O.R.E. System can change your life. It will let you manage your thoughts like a true champion. It is the answer to why a great or bad performance happens. More important, the S.C.O.R.E. System will lead you to what you need to do to prevent the proverbial bad day and accelerate a good moment into a great day.

The S.C.O.R.E. System has five key elements. They are *Self-discipline, Concentration, Optimism, Relaxation,* and *Enjoyment.*

When these elements are locked in place at their highest level, the *Zone phenomenon* will appear. You are only as strong as its weakest link.

Why is this so difficult for most performers? It's because there are external and internal factors that come into play. I call these *S.C.O.R.E. Makers and Breakers.* They can attack self-discipline one minute and enjoyment the next, or they can influence all of the S.C.O.R.E. components simultaneously. If we allow it, they attract or repel the Zone in a matter of a second.

In the Information Age, we all have cell phones, fax machines, e-mail, and text messaging. These delivery mechanisms send Makers and Breakers with lightning speed. Most of us are very vulnerable to internal and external stimuli. This is because our subconscious mind is amenable to suggestion. People are sending you their own propaganda in a relentless stream. You will find that many of these suggestions are for the purpose of making you think, feel, and act as others want you to think—and in ways that are to their advantage. Study what is said. How often do you hear these kinds of thoughts?

You haven't got a chance.
It's no use.
We can't win for losing.
I figured that would happen.
That's par for the course.
That's just the way it is.
I'm getting sick. Everybody is getting the flu.

These thoughts weaken our energy. They repel the Zone and pull us back into self-doubt. These are all potential S.C.O.R.E. Breakers.

How many times have you been immersed in the action of a movie and a cell phone rings? That's a S.C.O.R.E. Breaker. How about when you put on an outfit, and you feel great and look awesome, and then someone gives you the once-over and you pick up the vibe that you don't look so good? That's another S.C.O.R.E. Breaker.

You control what goes into the subconscious. You are the master filter. If you give your mental consent, a nonchampion's thought now becomes an action in your mind.

Here are two examples of S.C.O.R.E. Makers. Let's say you're playing golf. You slice a tee shot into the woods, it hits a tree, and bounces back on to the fairway. At that moment, you feel this is going to be a *great* day. Do you remember wanting to call someone for a date but were afraid to dial her number? You muster up some courage and get her on the phone, and she says, "I'm so glad you called. I've been thinking about you." Now that's a S.C.O.R.E. Maker.

There are a host of possible Breakers and Makers that can contribute to your performances fluctuating. Most of us meander our way to our goals. We can lose discipline, focus, confidence, relaxation, and fun in a blink of an eye. Staying on course in a straight line is not easy . . . especially if the goal or dream is lofty. Breakers can stop us in our tracks, and Makers can catapult us to great heights. You will soon learn how to combat the internal and external factors that always get in the way of the nonchampion.

To attract the Zone, you need to balance the five elements of S.C.O.R.E. What does this mean? Too little or too much of any element of S.C.O.R.E. will repel the Zone. You can possess self-discipline and concentration in school, but you may not enjoy the teacher's style and demeanor. This imbalance can cause you to learn at a slower rate. Or you may be extremely optimistic about reaching your dreams, but you have failed to create a disciplined pathway to your destination. This can cause frustration and disappointment. And many times I've even seen optimistic performers stumble because they tried too hard. These examples of imbalance all repel the Zone. We allow S.C.O.R.E. Breakers to affect us. Immunizing yourself from Breakers is one of the marks of a true champion. And surrounding yourself with S.C.O.R.E. Makers will assist you in performing with equal amounts of S.C.O.R.E. Hanging out with positive people will do the trick. Performing as a true champion requires balance, and balance requires learning the five elements of S.C.O.R.E. Join me as we begin with the first ingredient for living, working, and playing in the Zone: self-discipline.

CHAPTER 3

Self-Discipline

Self-discipline is literally and figuratively the first component of the acronym S.C.O.R.E. and the S.C.O.R.E. System itself. It leads the way to the Zone. Self-discipline is the biggest stumbling block for most nonchampions. It will be the first step in reducing your thoughts to the level of a champion. Clarity, simplicity, and balance will follow.

Self-discipline is the willingness and commitment to stay with a task(s) to reach well-defined goals that lead to a vision. Repeat this definition several times to yourself. At any given time you possess a high or low level of self-discipline: it can fluctuate.

How is your self-discipline in your job? Are you disciplined before you get to work? Are you still disciplined throughout the day? Are you disciplined as a manager or boss? What your team thinks is a direct re-flection of how you think. You know your team is only as good as what they think when you're not there. You're in charge of helping them manage their thoughts. That's your responsibility. Your self-discipline will affect those around you: it's contagious.

How about your family? How is the self-discipline of your kids? You know, your kids are only as good as what they think when you're not around—say, when they are with friends at a movie or a party.

How about you and your nutrition or physical condition? The champion is usually only disciplined in one or two life arenas. It's tough to be disciplined in all areas of your life. I understand this. How-ever, the true champion creates pathways for each of their life arenas.

So let's get disciplined now!

EXERCISE #4

HIGHER GROUND

This is the first step in eliminating chaos and getting your life in the Zone. Take out a blank sheet of paper and draw a circle . . . one circle. You're going to have as many as nine circles when we're done, so make sure you leave room.

These circles represent your different life arenas. An arena could be your self, your mate, your job, or your finances. All of your thoughts are contained in these arenas. By isolating the major dimensions of your life this way, your thoughts will be easier to manage. You can take a mental inventory.

In the first circle, write the word Self.

This pertains to you: your nutrition, your body weight, your spiritu-ality, your philosophies, and your principles for living. It's how you are, how you feel, how you think. It's only you. It's not your spouse or mate. It's not your job or kids. It's just you.

In the next circle, I want you to write Spouse, Husband, Wife, or

Mate—*whichever one pertains to you. If you do not have a significant other, go on to the next arena.*

In another circle, (these do not touch; make them separate) write down Job. *This is your professional craft, your vocation, or your main source of income. If you have more than one job, use separate arenas.*

In another circle, write either Brother *or* Sister *if you have siblings. If you don't have any siblings, go on to the next arena.*

In the next circle, place the word Parent *if you have children. If you don't have any kids, go on to the next arena.*

Everyone is either a Son *or a* Daughter. *Put that in the next circle, even if your parents are deceased.*

In another circle, write Finances. *This will include all of your assets, equity in your home, 401k, stocks and bonds, checking account, or cash on hand. Everything you own is in this circle.*

In the next circle, write Friends. *These are your closest group of friends.*

In another circle, put a Hobby. *If you're not a pro golfer but love golf, put golf in that circle.*

Now put the piece of paper on the floor and stand up.

When I used to go out and play when I was little, my grandfather was always concerned about me being in the woods alone. I could be gone for a couple of hours. He always told me, "Jimmy, if you get lost, you need to go to higher ground. If you're not sure where you are in the woods, you need to climb a tree or go up on a hill. Go to the highest place so you can look and see where you've been and see where you need to go . . . so you can find your way home."

We can have so many thoughts in our minds that we can become lost. Chaos prevails. As you survey your life arenas, you've gone to a higher ground. You're looking down on your life.

Only from a higher ground can you objectively see your life. Here you can take mental inventory of your thoughts. Now you can see where you are going.

Each arena occupies your thoughts—as well as the thoughts of others. You have thoughts about your family and the future of your family. Thoughts about the fight you had last night with your spouse, or thoughts about a special project at work.

Inside each arena, you will write down your key people. Some are your coaches. They dictate the arena basics and lead most of the thoughts. For example, coaches in the family arena guide where, when, and what everyone else eats. They are influential in the dress, speech, and overall actions of the arena. Some coaches lead by example, and some lead with words and gestures. This arena can have cocoaches, such as your mom and dad. The children are the players who react to the coach or cocoaches.

You can be a coach at work in your regional division and just a player in the national office. You can be player to your mom or dad in your Son or Daughter arena. And when your parents become elderly, you become their coach.

The Spouse or Mate Arena is one of the most difficult arenas of all. That's because there has never been a championship team that had two equal coaches simultaneously. You will need to change gears in this arena to be successful. As you mentally or physically change arenas, know and understand that the roles can change.

Now, at the top of the arena page write the number 2,000. This represents the number of thoughts the average person has per day in all of their Arenas. On any given day, your 2,000 thoughts are divided over all of your arenas. They are *not* sprinkled evenly. Your thoughts change on a moment-to-moment basis, and typically are concentrated in the arena where you have the most pressing issues.

If there is a crisis at work, that's where your thoughts will go. If your kid brings home bad grades, that's where your thoughts go. If your favorite uncle passes away, that's where your thoughts go. If you're going through a divorce, that's where your thoughts go. And if you have a major project that's due, you know the arena that will command your attention.

Do you worry? Which arena worries you the most? Worries occur when a thought that is anchored in the past projects itself into the future. It can even magnify itself as you envision what's ahead of you. This causes negative stress. Which of your arenas give you the most negative thoughts?

Let's examine the arena of self. What are the typical thoughts you have? Are you always concerned about how you look? Do you have to ask everyone, "Do I look good? Do I look OK? Does this match?" You're suggesting to others that the thoughts about yourself are negative. By trimming away these nagging self-doubts, you begin thinking like a true champion.

Now consider your Family Arena. What are you thinking? Are you thinking about the future? Are you thinking in the past?

How are you going to reduce nonchampion thoughts in your life?

Remember, when you are thinking like a champion, you discipline yourself to have 1,100 to 1,300 thoughts per day. This eliminates much of the excess baggage of worry, gossip, anger, impatience, apathy, frustration, embarrassment, assumption, envy, and anxiety that can dominate our thoughts in every arena. To begin trimming away your unproductive thoughts, you must know which arena is requiring more attention than it deserves. You must understand which people you are allowing to control your past or future negative thoughts.

As you review your life arenas, you are looking at your life through a different pair of glasses. As you limit and change your thoughts in each arena, so too will your life begin to change.

Every week, check your life arenas by going to higher ground.

Your next three assignments are as follows:

1. Create a collection of visions for your life. See something positive in the future for *each* of your arenas.
2. Create no more than five goals with timelines that you will accomplish to reach the vision in each arena. Make the goals measurable.
3. Break the goal down into necessary action steps for reaching your goals and eventually fulfilling your vision.

The true champion has mastered all three of these assignments. Develop a daily routine where you visualize your ultimate goal, and the steps you will take to reach it. See each step of the goal in your mind's eye. This can be done during meditation, exercise, or a vigorous walk. As you go through this process, you will begin to condition your subconscious mind to operate on "automatic pilot." This can be particularly important during a "moment of truth" when your next move can decide the outcome of the performance. Champions use the visualization tool every day.

What is visualization?

First off, you have two minds. One is your conscious mind that houses your 2,000 thoughts. It operates with the five senses of sight, sound, touch, taste, and smell. It is open all of your waking hours. It has reasoning capabilities. It knows right from wrong.

Second, you possess a subconscious mind. This mind never closes. It operates 24/7. It does not reason. It controls the physical, emotional, and intuitive reaction to your thoughts. It controls all of your bodily functions, such as digestion, blood manufacture, cell repair, perspiration, and breathing. *It takes things literally.* "I am stupid" thoughts will produce "I am stupid" actions. That's because your subconscious mind does *not* know the difference between fantasy and reality.

In fact, when you wake up from a scary nightmare, your heart is racing. Your eyes are dilated. It was so real. You are sweating profusely because of the image of running to escape some danger. You look around your bedroom and see that there is nothing in the room. Your subconscious mind had the nightmare on your mental screen of space, and it reacted to it as if it was real. That's right. Your subconscious mind does not know the difference between fantasy and reality. This is why visualization works!

EXERCISE #5

VISION 101

Most people lack an overarching vision for their lives, not to mention a vision for each of their life arenas. In this exercise, set a vision for each of your individual arenas. Having a clear vision for your health and wellness, career, family, finances, hobbies, and friends is the main step to becoming a true champion. Shut your eyes. Take four or five deep breaths. Unhinge your jaw. Now visualize McDonald's. What do you see? Golden arches? French fries? Or a Big Mac? Can you smell the food? Can you taste it? This is visualization.

I've experienced three ways to visualize. From the attendees that have taken my seminars, I've found that over 84 percent saw an image through their own eyes as if they were an active participant. Thirteen percent saw themselves from above like they were on a movie set looking down on the action. Either of these is equally effective. Finally 3 percent had difficulty seeing anything in their mind's eye. If this is you, start with seeing colors in your mind. Then change the colors. Take small steps and be patient.

Select an object in the room or near vicinity. Look at it for a few seconds and then shut your eyes and keep the image in your mind's eye. When the object fades or goes away in your mind, open your eyes and try the exercise again. Once you have become proficient with holding objects in your mind, try changing the object in your mind. Turn it upside down. Move it in a circle. Change its color. Move it closer. Move it farther away.

Next, create something in your mind that is not physically in your presence. Choose a person. See him smile. See her laugh. Give him a hug. Feel her embrace. Smell his scent. Hear her laughter. Make it real.

Visualization has no boundaries or limitations. "See it as it will be" is your new mantra.

Peter Haleas had vision. When he became the chairman of the Bridgeview Bank Group in Chicago, he inherited a fledging bank with meager assets of $125 million. By using the power of visualization, he envisioned his bank becoming a $1.5 billion institution in five years. This vision woke him up in the morning and put him to bed at night. He saw the pathway to this endeavor and relayed this vision and plan to his inner circle of coworkers. The entire bank committed to Peter's dream. With the power of visualization, the bank has passed the billion-dollar asset mark and is closing in on $1.5 billion.

A vision is something you see in your mind in the future. A Realtor can see a vibrant, flourishing section of town that is now a ghetto. A mother can see a straight-A student in her child that is struggling in school. A coach can see a superstar in a misguided talent that is barely surviving on the team. A teacher can see a future doctor in a delinquent child that never pays attention in class.

A vision is something you see six months from now or a year from now. An Olympic hopeful sees gold four years from now. You can call it a dream—the true champions I coach call it a vision.

EXERCISE #6

ADVANCED IMAGERY/VISUALIZATION

I teach four types of visualization, employing different types of images: task, situational, symbolic, *and* aftermath.

In task imagery, you visualize the same task over and over. Making a 10-foot putt a number of times in a row is a prime example. You can visualize the conclusion of a speech, closing a sale, or a making serve in tennis.

Situational imagery is the same as task imagery, but you have added conditions and circumstances. The same 10-foot putt is now set on the 18th green on the final day of the Masters in Augusta, Georgia.

Symbolic imagery is what comprises many of our dreams. Visualizing climbing over a 40-foot wall could symbolize overcoming a major obstacle in your life. Seeing a standing ovation with the crowds chanting your name can be used to bolster confidence and self-esteem. I have used symbolic imagery with all of my clients for over three decades.

Aftermath imagery is seldom used. It is "seeing" what happens after your vision or goals have been reached. Now what? What changes will take place? How will your family respond to your success? Will you change how you act? Will your relationships change? With aftermath imagery, you can dress-rehearse your successful journey. You can pre-

pare for life change in a positive way. This will keep a champion grounded and will let you thrive at the top. No flash in the pan success here.

Every champion that I have coached has had a vision. This vision wakes them up in the morning and puts them to bed at night.

So, what do you want? I ask every one of my clients, "What do you want out of your life?" Be concrete, I urge them: don't tell me happiness or lots of money. I need something that we can measure. Do you want to make a $100,000 salary? Do you want to be a millionaire? A billionaire? Do you want to move to a different city? Do you want a different job? Do you want to make a major-league baseball team? What do you want?

What is your vision for yourself—that is, the arena of self? It could be excellent health and wellness according to corresponding goals that you've set. These could be to have 8 percent body fat, or weigh 185 pounds, or wear a size 8 dress. What is your vision in your Finance Arena? Is it financial independence? What goals would reflect this? Net worth of $1 million? How about your Job Arena? President of your company? Can you see your kids going off to college, getting married, having a great life? Have you played that movie in your mind? Do you see them as successful, or do you see them as procrastinators or underachievers? What are your thoughts of the future in all your arenas?

Now, select a vision for each of your arenas. Don't forget that your thoughts are readable. Even though they are contained in your head, they are readable by others. Most champions only have a vision in one arena. The true champion has a vision in each of the arenas of her life.

In 2001, Alex Rodriguez signed a $252 million contract with the baseball team Texas Rangers. In addition to using the S.C.O.R.E. System, Alex used the tools of visualization, and with it he became the highest-paid athlete in the world. Here is how and why it worked for him—and how it will work for you.

When I first met Alex in the spring of 1996, he was playing short-stop for the Seattle Mariners. I asked him, "What do you want and why am I here?" He looked me cold in the eye and without hesitating said, "Hall of Fame." Now, you can measure that. He's either going to be inducted or not when his career ends. And I said, "Really? You're willing to pay for it?" He thought I was talking about my fee, and I said, "No, you're going to have to pay in time, energy, and thoughts you'll have to sacrifice. It's going to cost a lot."

All great accomplishments have a price. It's the price of thinking differently than everyone else. (Be aware that this can be upsetting to friends, family, and coworkers.)

Alex Rodriguez had an abnormal master vision, but his current statistics were below average. In fact, his batting average was one of the lowest in Major League Baseball at the time I met him. Here's what he did.

On April 18, 1996, in a downtown Milwaukee hotel, Alex envisioned three goals. Collectively, they would place him on the pathway to his dream. First, he saw himself winning the

> *All great accomplishments have a price. It's the price of thinking differently than everyone else. (Be aware that this can be upsetting to friends, family, and coworkers.)*

batting title at the end of year. He took possession of it in his mind. He saw it. He felt it. Next, he saw himself being selected to the 1996 all-star team within 90 days. He even saw his childhood idol, Baltimore Orioles great Cal Ripken Jr., walk up to him at the All-Star Game. Alex envisioned walking on the field and Ripken approaching him and saying, "Hi, my name is Cal Ripken Jr. I couldn't wait to meet you. I've heard so much about you." Finally, he envisioned in his mind being introduced on a late-night talk show as the new base-ball superstar. These three visions were examples of situational imagery.

Break down each vision into smaller goals. Imagination is only one part. It's crucial. It's important. But once you've made an investment in the future, the work really begins.

SETTING GOALS

Setting appropriate goals that fit nicely within your vision is an art form. Goals with timelines create the stress necessary to attract the Zone. For example, if your vision is to be a Hall of Fame baseball player, break it down into annual goals, such as hitting .300, having less than 10 errors a season, and blasting 30 home runs every year. These are the standards I need to meet to fulfill my vision.

Create no more than five goals with timelines that you will accomplish in each arena. Make the goals measurable. These goals create a positive stress that motivates and inspires you. If your visions are powerful and real and they are something you need in your life, then the goals will be easier to attain.

Inside each arena circle, write your goals. Review them weekly.

The next day, Alex woke up ready to treat himself as the batting champion. He set subgoals of hits and base on balls for each month and week. With his new mind-set, his batting average began to rise until it was the highest in the league. He was selected for the all-star team. As he walked on the field in his very first All-Star Game, his childhood idol, Cal Ripken Jr., the same man who was on a poster above his bed back in Miami, walked up to him and said, "Hi, my name is Cal Ripken Jr. I couldn't wait to meet you. I've heard so much about you." The exact same words he had heard in his mind back in April. He phoned me from the field in awe of the power of his vision.

In August, as he drove in a limousine through downtown Manhattan on his way to the *Late Show with David Letterman,* to be introduced as the game's new superstar, he said. "This is so weird. I've done this before." Yes, he did win the batting title in 1996.

Is it that easy? First, you must have the potential to reach your vision. And you need to commit to breaking it down into goals and daily routines or tasks.

<hr>

EXERCISE #8

ACTION STEPS

Breaking the goal down even further is the next step. Tasks are the necessary action steps for reaching your goals and eventually fulfilling your vision. For example, if my goal is to lose 20 pounds, then my tasks may include joining a gym, running one mile every day, or consuming 1,400 calories per day. What action steps to you need to take daily to reach your goals and vision? List no more than three tasks for each goal.

Action steps that are repeated daily, weekly, or monthly are called routines. These routines are performed before a performance, during a performance, or after a performance. They can be taken to any location and performed under any circumstance or condition. Familiarity breeds success. Routines will keep you on track with confidence toward your goal and vision pursuit.

<hr>

EXERCISE #9

THE ESSENCE OF YOUR CRAFT

This exercise begins with thinking about what you do for a living. What is the essence of your craft? A pitcher in baseball throws baseballs to well-defined targets with late-breaking good stuff. A professional golfer places a golf ball into 18 cups with the least amount of strokes. A car salesperson motivates people in improving their quality of transportation at a price they can afford.

*In each arena, know the essence of the craft. As a spouse, we en-
hance the other person mentally, spiritually, emotionally, and intellec-
tually. With this in mind, your thinking should be "You and I together
equal more than I apart." Walk through your arenas and understand
the essence of the craft in performing your best.*

Alex broke his vision down to only one thing. I asked him, "What do
you do for a living?" He said, "I play baseball." "Yes, but that is not the
essence of your craft," I replied. He said, "I hit home runs." No. "I
score runs so my team can win." No. I said, "You hit the core of the
ball with the sweet spot of your bat with an accelerated barrel. You hit
solid! That is the essence of your craft. When the ball is struck solid, it
gives the defense less time to get to the ball. Home runs, runs scored,
and victories will follow." Since 1996, he has thought, "I hit solid," before every game. Every game! Task imagery at its finest.

The great champion sees it as it will be. He takes possession of his
dreams. He makes them real. Once you've taken possession of your
dream, you need to walk the walk and talk the talk. You need to attract
the phenomenon called the Zone.

Self-discipline is the willingness and commitment to stay with the task(s) to reach well-defined goals that lead to a vision.

In 1996, Alex Rodriguez became self-disciplined. He had free will. He
was committed. He had a vision. He had goals and corresponding
daily routines.

He placed good stress on himself on his terms and conditions. He
was in control of his thoughts. This is essential.

Visualization will be one of your primary tools in becoming successful. Why? Because it programs the subconscious mind. Make it
real! With repetition, you can change your belief and expectation in
making your vision come true. When this happens, your subcon-

scious mind will manifest itself (behind the scenes) into the physical equivalent as if it is so. It will cause synchronicity, coincidence, and luck.

If you think you are poor, a victim of poverty, or a victim of conditions and circumstance, your subconscious will keep you shackled to this reality. Money will slip through your fingers. Opportunities will go unnoticed. If you think you are fat, your subconscious mind will reinforce the behaviors that keep you overweight. Nonchampions visualize negatives. Their days are generalized. Mistake tolerance is very low. The rhythm of the day is dictated by S.C.O.R.E. Breakers. There is a tendency to procrastinate. This person can easily quit or give up. The arenas in their life are complicated and overlap. You can be disciplined for a day and undisciplined the next. You can be disciplined in one Arena and totally undisciplined in another.

A true champion has a high level of self-discipline. This person has a clear vision in each of her arenas. The vision is very real in her mind-set with corresponding goals that have timelines. This person is patient. Actions and movements are simple and direct. The self-disciplined performer is in control and has reason over emotion. Likewise, the true champion is disciplined in thinking positively. She believes and expects that good fortune will happen. She is rarely disappointed. Self-discipline is the *willingness* and *commitment* to stay with the *task(s)* to reach very well-defined *goals* that lead to a *vision*.

You have free will. You can choose any thought or reject any thought. You can plan for the future, adjust your thoughts when in the present tense, and reflect on the past for learning purposes or enjoyment. This concept is your choice.

The champion *chooses* his vision and breaks it down into smaller tasks that lead to well-defined goals and ultimately long-term vision. He is armed with a strategy and corresponding tactics. He is prepared for possible adversity. Without a plan, your dreams are only wishful thinking. That is the mind-set of the nonchampion.

You must make a commitment.

The champion illuminates a *committed* pathway that moves to the vision. You must "see" the pathway to your dreams. Second, commit to the daily tasks necessary for goal attainment. Most nonchampions stumble here. They lack both vision and commitment. However, the true champion has a vision, goals, and tasks for *every* life arena.

Finally, you need to be relentless in your pursuit of excellence. We all will fall off the pathway to the Zone and must know how to get back in balance.

Success is getting up one more time from defeat.

It's never-ending. Being disciplined while in a performance is paramount in reaching goals. Regaining your discipline in a performance is the mark of the champion. Here is your final assignment in this chapter.

EXERCISE #10

THE DAILY DRESS REHEARSAL

This exercise is a great way to foster your self-discipline. It's called the Daily Dress Rehearsal. Choose the arena that needs the most self-discipline. Most people select the work arena.

Let's go to the end of your day. Before you walk out the door, take out a blank piece of paper. Write down a minimum of three (maximum of five) tasks that you want to accomplish by the end of the next day. Make sure these tasks move the needle closer to obtaining your goals and vision—no "busy" work. Then perform a mental dress rehearsal: Shut your eyes. Relax your body. Unhinge your jaw. Now see in your mind's eye how these tasks will be accomplished. See them through to completion. See them executed while being in the Zone. Open your eyes. Turn the paper over and go to your next arena.

The next morning when you wake up, you've already performed a dress rehearsal for the day. When you get to work, start attacking the list that you made the day before. You don't have to figure out what to do; just get in the now and do it. At the end of the day, throw away yesterday's piece of paper and begin a new list for the next day. Perform another dress rehearsal in your mind and repeat this process daily. If a task is written down more than three days in a row, do one of the following:

1. *Delete the task entirely.*
2. *Delegate or transfer the task to someone else.*
3. DO THE TASK IMMEDIATELY WITHOUT FURTHER PROCRASTINATION!

Self-discipline is the willingness and commitment to stay with a task(s) to reach well-defined goals that lead to your vision.

How is your S level?

CHAPTER 4

Concentration

The second intangible in the S.C.O.R.E. chain is concentration. Many people have a lifetime of dreams, goals, and great ideas that go nowhere. Their lack of focus has kept many of these potential champions on the sidelines.

Concentration is the ability to focus mental and physical energy on the task(s) to reach well-defined goals that lead to a vision. Commit this definition to memory.

Why is the C second in the S.C.O.R.E. chain? In order to concentrate at an optimum, you must have a specific destination to direct your energy. That is why S, with its disciplined vision and corresponding goals, is first. Most of us are scattered. Our minds race from one thought to another.

However, a champion has the ability to focus for extended periods of time until their goals are met. With no worry of the future and no pain from the past, he can laser his mental and physical energies to well-defined targets. When this energy is channeled, it can cut through all obstacles.

When my client Luke Donald, a PGA touring professional, is preparing to hit an approach shot to the green, he narrows his field of vision to this image: "I hit solid to the hula-hoop-size target in the middle of the green." *You never see the bunkers, trees, or water hazard until you take your eye off the target.*

With the vision tucked under the arm and the dress rehearsal complete, the champion walks into the arena ready to detach from the results of the past and unknowns of the future. This is the champion's mantra:

I have no future. I have no past.
My goal is to make the present last.
I'm in the now!

This is why a person with high concentration has specific goals and corresponding daily tasks in her life. And when she performs, she engages her mind in the moment. She performs in the here and now. She is not easily distracted by S.C.O.R.E. Breakers. Here's what I mean.

EXERCISE #11

A LESSON IN CONCENTRATION: THE CHEETAH

The cheetah quietly crawls through the tall grassland on the hunt for its dinner. It hasn't eaten in days. Slowly, it edges into a clearing where a herd of impala nervously graze. Ever so stealthily, the lean predator eyes his prey. From the large group of mild-mannered animals, she selects a single victim. The cheetah's energy is piercing and locked. She targets the exposed jugular of her dinner-to-be. With the swiftness of a blur, the jungle cat springs into the clearing. The terrified herd scatters in panic. A pregnant impala falls in the path of the charging cheetah—an easy victory.

Suddenly, an amazing thing occurs. Instead of stopping, the cat leaps over the fallen mother-to-be and continues the pursuit of her original selection. She passed up more than a half dozen impala because she wants the biggest of the herd, the largest prize. Soon, with speed and tenacity, the hunt is over. Victory. The largest impala is under her claws.

This is focus. This is single-mindedness. This is the epitome of not going where the grass is greener. The cheetah could easily have changed prey in the middle of the hunt. No. The predator's mind was set. One purpose. One focus. This is the ultimate form of concentration.

Luckily, we do not have to hunt in the grasslands or jungle for our next dinner. But we do hunt for sales, grades, better relationships, and better opportunities. We hunt for personal records and good fortune. We are hunters. And a better quality of life is our ultimate prey.

In this exercise, I want you be the cheetah. Pick something that you have been procrastinating. Be sure it's not too big of a project. It could be the huge pile of laundry, the dirty garage you wanted to clean for the past two months, or the ceiling light you've been meaning to fix. Pick something that would take at least 30 to 60 minutes of focus. Choose the project and do it now! Do not stop until it's done. No phone calls. No television breaks. No distractions. Like the cheetah, choose to have an unwavering focus. This is your exercise in concentration.

Are you focused on opportunity? But how can you see opportunity if you're not prepared? Sometimes it knocks very softly. If you're worried about the past, you'll miss it. If you're anxious for the future, you'll never know opportunity was near. You must be ready. You must be ready to focus.

Does the cheetah worry, "Maybe the impala is too fast," or "What if I get hurt?" or "Which one will I catch?" No. The cheetah gets her goal.

Nonchampions chase the whole herd and catch nothing. They race after a multitude of ideas and hope one works. That's not the cheetah. The cheetah would go hungry with this mind-set.

Hunters that stay in the present see options when others are blind. They know how to seize the moment. They are focused. No "coulda', shoulda', woulda', gotta, gonna" in their vocabulary. "I am!" I can!" This is a great hunter's thought.

When selling, focus on the buyer. He's telling you if he's uncomfortable with your pitch. He's telling you if he's not confident with your service or product. He's telling you his needs. Focus on them. He's telling you he's buying. So quit selling and close the deal!

When playing tennis, focus on the ball as it leaves your opponent's racket. Focus on your foe scrambling for your deep corner drive. Anticipate the weak return and pounce on it in the air for an easy volley into the open court. The opposition feels the focus of the champion.

In your Self Arena, losing weight is a challenge for most of us. Focus on what you eat. Nothing enters your body without your permission. Plan your intake one day at a time. See tomorrow's meals before you wake up. Then pay attention to the size of your meal. Put blinders on to get you through the day with the intake you choose. Focus like the cheetah. One meal at a time. Try this exercise.

EXERCISE #12

THE LASER

There are three ways we view the world as we perform: broad vision, tunnel vision, *and* Zone vision. *We spend most of our days using broad vision, only choosing tunnel and Zone vision when we need to lock in on an urgent objective. In broad vision, we see everything at once, but noth-*

ing specific. We are oblivious to details. The majority of our day is spent here. Next is tunnel vision. When we need to make a birdie putt, we can narrow our focus in tunnel vision to get the job done. In this vision, we are not easily disturbed.

But we really want to see with Zone vision, where your eyes double or triple their shutter speed to give you the illusion that everything is in slow motion or the objects are larger than normal. Many of my baseball clients have experienced this phenomenon.

On May 2, 2002, Mike Cameron, center fielder for the Seattle Mariners, became one of only 13 men to hit four home runs in one major league game. He told me. "It was like magic. The ball seemed in slow motion. It looked like a grapefruit. My eyes were lasers." That was Zone vision. The laser exercise will show you how to narrow your focus and induce tunnel and Zone vision.

Wad up a piece of paper into a ball. Stand five to seven feet away from a cup, bowl, or wastebasket. Using your opposite hand, I want you to toss the ball into the opening two times in a row. This will require you to narrow your focus.

Before you begin shut your eyes, unhinge your jaw slightly and visualize seeing the ball go in the cup. Hear the sound in your mind of the ball hitting your target. Performing this exercise with high concentration will require you to choose a toothpick-size target inside the cup, bowl, or basket.

Make a small possible circle with your index finger and thumb. Now reduce the circle as small as you can. Look through this opening at your target. The smaller the target, the easier it is to focus your energy. Now soften your eyes . . . do not strain . . . lock in on the toothpick-size target.

If you miss, act like nothing happened. Do not judge. Do not analyze. Do not even roll your eyes in reaction to your miss. Just trust your subconscious and keep throwing to the target. Your subconscious has the ability to make adjustments as long as you tell it exactly what you want. Detach from the outcome. Focus on execution only. After a half *dozen misses, you may change tactics. Increase your trajectory. Toss with more softness. That's OK. Get the job done. Once you've accomplished the task, can you apply the same exercise to your life?*

How do I focus on each performance? This next exercise will show you how. It's a technique called *framing*.

<hr>

EXERCISE #13

FRAMING

Every performance has a beginning, middle, and an end. Framing is the art of opening and closing performances with focused energy. Framing can be executed for the whole year. See the beginning and see the end. Start the first quarter of the year with a plan and deliver energy to your performances. Most people have New Year's resolutions that usually fizzle out about this time. Then finish the year on your terms. Close the last three months with purpose and conviction. Months, weeks, and days can all be framed like this.

Make up your mind that you will wake up positive and go to bed positive. This is framing your days.

Now frame your performances. When giving a speech, open with purpose and enthusiasm while engaging the audience with your energy. Practice your opening. Know how you will walk onstage. Finally, close the performance with the understanding of what you want the audience to think once they drive away in their cars. Close with positive energy and enthusiasm. Know how you will get offstage. This is framing.

This happened to two PGA Tour golfers I coached. They both shoot 71. One is happy and one is upset. The first golfer is playing poorly all day until the last three holes. Finally, three birdies in a row leave this person smiling. The other golfer is having an awesome round—until the last three holes. Two straight bogies and a double bogie leave a bad taste in his mouth with thoughts of shoulda', coulda', and woulda' lingering into the next day's performance.

Open like a champion. Close like a champion. Do this in your life and not just your sport. For example, say hello like you mean it and say good-bye with enthusiasm and high energy. Enter your office with a smile and a plan for the day. Greet your team with consistent positives. Leave your office with the same mind-set regardless of the outcome from your day.

Frame your introductory meetings. The next time you meet someone new, look him in the eye long enough during the introduction to discern his eye color. Don't stare. Just momentarily engage with your energy. When that person says his name, repeat it back to him. If you don't feel comfortable doing that out loud, then just repeat it in your own mind. When you say good-bye, use his name again. Leave him with a piece of your positive energy.

Send your energy when you arrive and leave some behind when you leave. This is how I want you to enter and exit your life arenas.

Your next exercise is about awareness focusing.

<hr>

EXERCISE #14

AWARENESS FOCUSING

I want you to read the body language of the people you see in the next 24 hours. Be in the now. Talk less and listen and look more. Focus your energy on what people are saying and how they say it. Listen for negative words. Be aware of any judgmental talk. Notice anyone acting or talking like a victim. This especially happens when the weather is bad: "Ugh, I hate going out in this rain."

Tomorrow, with your concentration heightened, you will become even more aware of the champions and nonchampions. Be in the now.

Engage all of the five senses into what you're doing. If you are a salesperson walking into an office to make a presentation, mentally and

Remember: Concentration is focusing all of your mental and physical energy.

physically engage with each person. Then take a mental picture of the room. See all the pictures on the wall and notice the people, places, and things in the frames. Swiftly focus on the items on the desk. This focused awareness will pick up information that you can use later in your presentation. Know that everything in the room is near and dear to the person sitting behind the desk. Use those items sometime during the presentation to make a mental connection with the prospective buyer. And when exiting the office, focus on the body language of each person as you say good-bye.

Now that the meeting is over, give yourself a mental quiz. Did you remember everyone's name and title? Were they disciplined and focused on what you were saying? What did you learn from the physical aspects of the office? What did the pictures on the wall reveal? Was the meeting positive or negative? What call to action do you need to perform? Rate your overall awareness focusing.

This next exercise will help you focus on what really matters.

THE 90-SECOND RULE

Use the 90-second rule before every arena change. For example, suppose you have been away from people that you care about, such as family and close friends, for at least two hours. The first 90 seconds that you see them has more impact than spending hours with them later. How many times have we gone home from a hard, long day at work and dismissed the ones we care for upon arrival? "I'm too tired. Not now, I want to rest first." How about when we say nothing at all? How many times have you been greeted at the door and you were not aware of the mood or disposition of the greeter?

The next time you go home after an absence of two or more hours, prepare yourself to give your family and or friends your undivided attention for the first 90 seconds. You may have to make that last cell phone call in the driveway, or you may need to clear your brain for a few minutes before you walk through the door. Be prepared as you enter a new life arena. Visualize seeing the people in the arena as vibrant, happy, and smiling. Then, for the first 90 seconds, give all your undivided attention and energy to the greeting. Your attentive words and actions say, "I love you . . . I missed you . . . I value you . . . I need you in my life." This will make a difference in the lives of those you love.

The 90-second rule works at the office, home, or anywhere you care about people. Start using the 90-second rule in your life. If you don't use it, the next thing you know, no one will be waiting at the door — not even the dog.

A true champion with high concentration is accurate, productive, and efficient. His energies are directed outward. He performs with no internal or external distractions. He is immunized from S.C.O.R.E. Breakers. He completes each task before he moves on to the next.

A nonchampion has too many goals and too many tasks. This leads to distraction, to his energy getting spread too thin, and therefore being overwhelmed by problems. Getting caught up in worries about the past or the future can both become S.C.O.R.E. Breakers.

Low concentration spawns inefficiency, missed opportunity, and a loss of overall energy. As our concentration drops, we leave the door open for self-doubt, confusion, and chaos. Most of the time, our concentration wanes because we take on too much. Computers slow down or freeze when there are too many programs open simultaneously. We perform the same way when we attempt to tackle too many projects at once.

As energy is spread too thin, awareness of not getting the job done causes another dangerous energy change. Low C performers slowly shift their energy from goals and targets to themselves. They talk about themselves too much. They think of problems as opposed to solutions. They complain like victims. They make generalized judgments about other people. They question their own techniques. They question their judgment. The energy of a low C performer is used in introspection instead of attacking solutions. This overanalysis will cause a loss of speed, quickness, and efficiency. This results in competitors bypassing them as their energy weakens. Even if the performer regains their focus, this lull can be enough to negatively impact the outcome of the performance.

This nonchampion can even have too much concentration. Many people force the action. They try too hard. You can see the brow of these performers furrow and their eyes squint as they try to make something happen. This forced focus results in a loss of relaxation. This will cause the performance level to drop.

Concentration is the ability to focus mental and physical energy on the task(s) to reach well-defined goals that lead to a vision.

You've set your goals. Attack them one at a time. Send them your energy. Get in the now! Be the cheetah! How's your concentration level?

CHAPTER 5

Optimism

"I'm king of the world!" When Leonardo DiCaprio yelled this affirmation from the top of the ill-fated *Titanic*, it epitomized the ultimate in optimism. He expressed belief, expectancy, and confidence in his life. He thought it. He felt it.

Young Cassius Clay leaped to the top rope of the ring apron and proclaimed, "I *am* the greatest!" This moment in sports history occurred after he defeated world heavyweight boxing champion Sonny Liston for the title. Decades later, we still revere older Muhammad Ali for his supreme confidence, belief, and expectancy. Optimism is part of his extraordinary legacy.

Optimism is the cornerstone of the S.C.O.R.E. System; it is literally and figuratively at the heart and core of the word S.C.O.R.E. and the System itself. Optimism is where a champion finds strength, especially during tough times. It can withstand the weight of shifting conditions and circumstances, and build a champion's drive to overcome seemingly insurmountable odds. It can level the playing field for the titans of industry and the mom-and-pop start-up. It leaves an open crack in the door of opportunity for the true believer.

Before I relate my optimistic view about the power of optimism, I must warn you: protect this part of you at all costs. Be aware of your O level. It can be undermined with lightning speed. If not prepared, your optimism level can change from a positive to a negative vis-à-vis a dirty look, an e-mail, or a phone call. It can curl up and shrink like bacon on a stove—and in less time. Just like that, you can become deflated. De-energized. Doubt will drape you. A fog of chaos will roll in. Arenas will overlap. Negative thoughts will surface, each gaining strength and speed in geometric proportion. Thinking about problems becomes the problem. Putting out fires becomes commonplace. An outgoing person will become silent. A smile will turn upside down. A bold performance will grow meek. A magnetic personality will have no pull. Your imagination will turn against you. Positive belief and expectancy will abandon ship. When your O level crumbles, it can have an adverse effect on all other components of S.C.O.R.E. And this change can occur with blinding speed. This is *not* the direction of the champion. Beware of the danger signs.

True champions never waver in their inner optimism. Boosting optimism inflates our Self-discipline, Concentration, Relaxation, and definitely Enjoyment like air going into the tires of an Indy car on race day. The inner feelings of superiority, dominance, and knowing flowing from optimism will literally change your physical look on the outside.

A high level of optimism pushes the limits of possibility and walks through the door of opportunity. Care for it every day of your life.

Your optimism level during any performance reflects your high or low level of confidence, trust, faith, hope, and positive self-esteem. You will possess the feeling of I can, I will, and I know.

Commit this definition to memory: *Optimism, or O, is the belief and expectancy that one can execute the task(s) to reach well-defined goals that lead to a vision.*

Do you know the deadly effects of negativity—the absence of optimism? Negative people speak with cynicism, give up easily, and think and act like victims. They tend to judge. Sarcasm is their verbal style. "If I didn't have any bad luck, I wouldn't have any luck at all," they announce. They suck the life force out of everyone they're around. This is *not* optimism. This is *not* the mind-set of a champion.

The optimism of a champion and a true champion is obvious. You can feel his positive energy. You know he believes in himself. He commands your attention. His head is up and his posture is erect. He speaks in positives. Champions have a supreme belief and expectancy that they *will* succeed. In a crisis, they have the ability to be silent while exuding confidence with no spoken words.

However, true champions go beyond belief. They go beyond expectancy. They enter the realm of knowing. They know what they do today will lead them on the pathway to goal attainment and ultimately their vision. They are confident. And they look confident because they know they are the best-prepared performer. The true champion wins first in his mind, then walks into the arena . . . every arena. He is prepared to open the performance on his terms. He is prepared to make adjustments regardless of the conditions or circumstances. He trusts his intuition. He expects results. And he is prepared to close the performance with authority. Everyone else enters the arena, and then tries to figure out what to do, where to go, and how to do it.

Optimism *is* the fulcrum of your S.C.O.R.E. Level. It's at the heart and soul of the true champion.

KEEP YOUR CHIN UP

Right now, I want you to do something I will never ask you to do again. First, shut your eyes. Now I want you to place a negative image in your mind. Hold that thought. Next, I want you to put your head down on your chest or your sternum. Drop your head and hold the negative thought. Make it real. Make it vivid. I want you to see and feel whatever you're thinking.

Now, with the same negative thought, raise your head up, above the parallel point. Put your chin up high and see if you can hold that same negative thought. With the negative thought still in your mind, drop your head again. Continue to raise and lower your head several more times while maintaining the negative thought. More than 80 percent of my seminar students have a difficult time keeping the negative thought clear in their mind with their chin up above the parallel point. However, with your head down, negatives will rush into your brain with incredible clarity. For those who seek to be true champions, we need to make a rule right here, right now. No one drops their head. I repeat, "No one drops their head!" It's not acceptable — especially when something doesn't go your way. Talk and walk with optimism. Mom was right. Keep your chin up!

Your exercise over the next week is to walk with your posture erect and your head held high. See how you feel at the end of the day. I'll bet that you are more positive, upbeat, and confident, thus increasing your optimism level.

With your head and chin high and your gait fast-paced and positive, it's now time to talk the talk.

POSITIVE SELF-TALK

How you speak to yourself has a direct impact on programming your subconscious mind. You know this now. "I am stupid" statements do cause "I am stupid" actions. Remember: your subconscious mind takes your statements literally.

It is not necessarily the words that are damaging as much as the image projected by the words on the screen of space in your mind. For example, is the following statement positive? "I'm going to lose weight." The answer is a resounding no. *The image placed in your mind is of someone who needs to lose weight. Since the subconscious takes the words literally, it keeps you fat so you can lose weight in the future. To be true to this, it will keep you from losing weight now. Did you follow that? It's better to say, "I'm thin," while placing an image of your thin body in your mind.*

This is called an affirmation. Now you know how it works. Every all-star baseball player I've coached has used the same affirmation. I hit solid. I hit solid. *This statement conjures up the image of striking a baseball solid with an accelerated bat head. This image has sound and feeling of solid contact.*

An affirmation can be a statement or just a single word. It is the image that is placed on your mental screen that counts. Use affirmations directed to problem solving or goal reaching, such as "I'm a millionaire," or just the word millionaire. *"I'm number one" or just "number one." "I am thin" or just the word* thin. *These statements or words backed with belief and expectancy repeated over and over will impact the subconscious mind.*

Now, let's change how we meet people. I want you to review and, if needed, alter the way you say hello and good-bye to everyone

Change is made with affirmations.

you meet, especially when people ask, "How are you?" Most of us reflect the mood of our current environment, condition, or circumstance. We tend to react to each person we greet according to his mood or demeanor. Now I want you to react according to *you*. Positive . . . bold . . . confident . . . a Champion.

<hr>

EXERCISE #18

UPGRADE YOUR HELLO AND GOOD-BYE

Most of us greet friends, family and strangers the same way: "Hi." "How are you?" "What's up?" We take this greeting for granted. Champions bring a higher level of energy and optimism to their greeting and salutation. I mean it! When someone greets you with "How are you?" reply: "Awesome!" "Great!" "Fantastic!" You choose the greeting. Make it simple. Mix it up. But by all means be consistent. When you say goodbye, leave the person or group with a positive, energetic farewell: "Godspeed." "Be safe." "See you soon." This is simple. Make it part of your every day. Be consistent. Mean what you say. And let the people you know feel the difference.

Yes, as you read this book, you are walking the walk and talking the talk—at least for a little while. How do you keep this demeanor over the long term? How can you keep your head up three months from now, especially if things aren't going well? How can you continue with your positive affirmations on a repetitive basis? How can you greet everyone as a champion? *It depends on the power of your vision.* Does it wake you up in the morning? Does it put you to bed at night?

What's next is crucial. Your subconscious mind, which controls your body language as well as your intuition, is most fertile for suggestion and change at two different natural times during a 24-hour cycle. It's at these times that your brain produces alpha brain waves. This occurs just before you fall into a REM, or rapid eye movement deep sleep, and just as you come out of it (just before you aw

Although this fertile state of mind can be induced by relaxation ⌐ meditation techniques, the times before sleep and after you awake are the easiest times to embed the power of your vision and goals. The true champion knows this. When you go to sleep tonight, select one arena vision and see it in your mind as if it were so. See it accomplished in a finished

> ***What you think before you sleep and as you awake has more impact on programming your subconscious for success or failure than at any other natural time.***

state. When you awake tomorrow morning before you get out of bed, repeat the exact same visualization. Once you perform this ten days in a row, you are on your way to making serious change. This works! *Period!*

I remember living in a two-bedroom home in the hills of the Appalachian Mountains in eastern Kentucky with my mom, my dad, and my dog, Spot. In my bedroom, the termites had eaten most of the floor. There was just enough wood for the bed to stay off the ground. My dad made a wooden plank that I could walk from my bed to the other parts of the house. I didn't realize it, but times were financially tough for us.

I asked my mom at the time, "Are we poor?" She replied, "Absolutely not! Is this because of your bedroom? In fact, you have the greatest bedroom ever." I said, "I do?" With the wisdom of a prophet she said, "Yeah, you can be anything you want to be in this bedroom. You can walk the plank like on a pirate ship. Use your imagination. And you can walk a tightrope in the circus as you go from the bed to the other rooms. In fact, you have your own room, unlike the Botts brothers up the road. They have to share." Then she laughed. "Also, you don't have to take Spot outside. He can come and go as he pleases." (Some nights I could see Spot's eyes in the dark, below where the floor used to be. At least I always hoped it was Spot.) "By walking on this plank every day you'll have the best balance of any ballplayer around," Mom said. "You're not poor. You're rich." Most nights my mother would enter my bedroom as I drifted off to sleep. Touching my forehead, she would whisper softly, "I believe in you." Then she would tuck me in and leave the room. In reality, we were in poverty, but I never knew it. I always thought I was wealthy. And so, by the age of five, I felt wealthy. Very soon I believed in me.

EXERCISE #19

I BELIEVE IN ME

Just before you go to sleep tonight, try this very simple exercise. With your eyes shut, jaw unhinged, and tongue relaxed, repeat silently to yourself, "I . . . believe . . . in . . . me." Place silence between the words. Say it as if it's so. Say it slowly with passion. "I . . . believe . . . in . . . me." Say this ten times in a row. You'll know when you've connected to your inner self. Inside your mind, you'll see and feel an illumination. Try it. You'll see.

Back in the late 1970s, I was coaching one of the top-ranked tennis players in the world. We went to a tournament in San Francisco in which the number one and number two players in the world were not going to play. So my guy was "the man." The promoter loved us. We were treated great—limos, suites, the works. Everything was awesome. During the first three rounds, Italian Adriano Panatta won easily. Now he was in the quarterfinals, playing one of the newcomers on the ATP Tour. "What's the problem?" I thought. "He's not top-ranked. This next opponent has never won a major. What's the big deal? I'm coaching the former French Open champion, one of the top-ranked players in the world—*no problem.*"

As the match unfolded, this low-ranked, left-handed, red-headed jerk of a guy has no respect for a top-ranked player in the world. He stalls. He berates an umpire. He yells at a ball kid. He takes his racket and whacks all the heads off the flowers in a flower box by the court. However, he crushes my player! We are humiliated! On the pro tennis tour, when you lose, you cruise. We left San Francisco so fast we barely had time to pack our bags.

Fourteen years later, I'm at my home in Chicago having dinner with my best friend, Peter Fleming (who I coached for eight years on the ATP Tour), and his doubles partner, John McEnroe Jr. I turned to John that night and said, "Do you remember when I met you back in San Francisco?" He smirked and replied, "Oh, you mean when I crushed your Italian boy?" We all started laughing. And I said, "Yeah, Adriano Panatta. How did you do that? Your ranking was so low. How did you play like that?" McEnroe looked me cold in the eye and said, "I was number one in the world. My ranking just hadn't caught up yet." Wow! *You were number one in the world and your ranking had not caught up yet!* That's optimism! That's believing you're the best long before the awards, the accolades, or the pats on the back from the coach.

The optimistic performer embraces their vision long before the fame or fortune arrive. *You must be it long before you become it.*

I coached Bella International, the exclusive Honda distributor in Puerto Rico and one of the best-managed companies in North America. Their receptionist made $10 an hour. I walked up to her one day and said, "Would you like to make $30 an hour?" She said, "Absolutely." I said, "Will you come in an hour early every day? Will you leave an hour later, work on Saturdays (although I know that's your day off), and every now and then work on Sunday? And if we ask you to forgo your vacation this year, would you do all that for $30 an hour?" And she said, "Absolutely." Then I said, "Would you do all that I asked you

McEnroe looked me cold in the eye and said, "I was number one in the world. My ranking just hadn't caught up yet."

for $10 an hour?" She adamantly replied, "There's no way." And I responded, "That's why you'll never make $30 an hour."

If you want to be a $30-an-hour worker, you have to think as if you are at that level long before your boss is going to give it to you. You need to be a millionaire long before you make a million dollars. This tool called "think as if" is very powerful.

EXERCISE #20

THINK AS IF . . .

Just like John McEnroe, think as if you have completed your mission and fulfilled your vision. Project yourself into the future while using all of your five senses. If the vision is reached, how will you feel? How will you talk and act? How does the most organized homemaker in the world act? How does the greatest sales manager act when confronted with poor sales performance? "Act as if . . . until your vision and goals are reached.

How many times have you started your day with your optimism bank account overflowing with confidence, trust, belief, and expectancy? And how many times did you have it depleted by the day's end? This next tool will prevent that from happening. Adding this to your life will make *major* changes in your optimism.

EXERCISE #21

THE FIVE-SECOND RULE

Most of us are aware of the importance of preparation. Pre-performance routines are executed daily by the majority of professional athletes, sales executives, and managers. From mental and physical dress rehearsal to relaxation techniques, the peak performer prepares to enter a Zone state of mind. However, the truly great performers have another tool up their sleeve. It's the five-second rule. You are only as good as the five seconds after every performance. That's right—you are only as good as the five seconds after every performance. Once the performance has been completed, the next five seconds will provide an opportunity to make a deposit or a withdrawal from your bank account of optimism. For example, when you're playing golf, do you think of the missed putt after it lips out, or do you just clear your mind and hit your next tee shot? How many times in a round of golf do you judge your shots or feel like a victim of misjudgment or luck? The key to sustaining a Zone state is to not go back into the past. Every time you do, you have moved one step further from the Zone.

When you make an error or mistake in any endeavor, be prepared to do one of the following immediately after the performance.

1. *Act like it didn't happen. No thought. No judgment. No acting like a victim or judge.*
2. *Do it over correctly in your mind. (This is only good if time allows.)*
3. *Gather your energy for the next objective, target, or performance.*
4. *Make a deposit of positives. Say the desired results as if it's so. Use an affirmation.*

Again, this is all done within the five seconds after the performance. Preplan the tool you will employ. Prepare your mind for using the five-second rule. It is easy to be ambushed with the unexpected. Always make deposits in your optimism bank account.

The great performers do not violate the five-second rule. They make deposits. This is one of the major differences between the good performer and the champion.

Why do we beat ourselves up so much? Why do we sometimes put ourselves down? We know better, but we do it anyway. We learned to do this as little kids around the ages of four or five. This is the number one defense mechanism for human beings. We make a mistake, and we get scolded. We do it again, and we get yelled at. We do it again, and we get punished. Then we do it again, and this time within five seconds of the mishap, we yell at ourselves or berate ourselves. "I'm so stupid," "I'm such an idiot," we might say. We learn that if we beat ourselves up, then those we love won't. If we do it enough, we might even get sympathy or kind words, and that's all we wanted anyway.

I believe that consistent adherence to the five-second rule will help knock out this negative learned behavior.

A champion is the most optimistic person in the arena. The true champion is the most optimistic in *every* life arena. Believe you can do it. Expect things to work out for the best. Be confident. Trust your ability, and especially trust your intuition or instincts. Be determined. Treat yourself like a champion. Talk the talk and walk the walk.

Nonchampions, who have low optimism, have no energy in their voice or body language. Their eyes avoid contact. Verbal negatives abound. They can easily put themselves down. They say things like "I'm so fat" or "I hate when I do that" or "I'm such an idiot." Nonchampions definitely violate the five-second rule.

Nonchampions are unsure about their goals. They place too much emphasis on what other people think. They have little pride. And this can happen to the best of the best. Everything is relative.

As I traveled the world on the men's professional tennis tour, I was coaching seven players simultaneously ranked in the world's top 50. In the first year that the U.S. Open was played at Flushing Meadows, New York, I walked into the locker-room facility with my players. We arrived three days early to practice on the new courts. At the time, there were no assigned lockers for any of my players. They could locker anywhere they wanted. There were two locker rooms in the facility. One was very small, off to the left as you walked in. It could accommodate 16 players. The other was a cavernous room where the majority of the players would locker. I looked into the smaller room and waved my team to go in here. One by one, they looked inside. Only one walked through the door. Was it a coincidence that he was a French Open champion? Is that why he walked in and the rest refused? Six men of world-class stature wouldn't enter that locker room. And if you could've looked in there, you'd know why. Inside were

Champions hang out with champions.

great Arthur Ashe, Jimmy Connors, and Bjorn Borg, the greatest players in the world with the highest-possible ranking. Somehow they had sequestered themselves in that particular area of this clubhouse.

Mom was right again. Be careful with whom you associate. You're the mirror image of your friends and associates. I saw the same situation on the PGA Tour.

I coached a PGA golfer at the Masters. We were at Augusta National on the veranda overlooking the course. It was jammed with people. There was only one table available with two seats open. Two men were already there, engaged in conversation. I said, "Let's go sit over there." My client/student refused. He wouldn't go. Believing he was behind me, I walked to the open seats. He didn't follow. As I put down a little tray of food, I introduced myself and said, "Hi, I'm Jim Fannin." And the men at the table said, "I'm Jack Nicklaus." "I'm Gary Player." I said, "You guys mind if I sit here?" They said, "No, not at all." *Optimistic people hang out with optimistic people.*

Sometimes when your optimism level has taken a major blow, you might need to be a politician and start selling yourself on yourself. Let me explain.

<hr>

EXERCISE #22

SELL YOURSELF ON YOURSELF

Fifteen years ago, I experienced a month I'll never forget. I owned and operated a 60,000-square-foot sports and fitness center outside of Chi-

cago. As the sole investor, the financial burden of the club was squarely on my shoulders. After a written promise of refinancing fell through at the last minute. I was faced with the task of finding a new bank. How was this possible? "This had been organized for months," I thought. Yet here I was, faced with a serious dilemma. I didn't want a new bank. I needed one! Now!

With only thirty days until my current loan expired. I embarked on a quest for serious cash. The first banker I saw laughed at the proposition. "You want what? When? That's not possible," he replied. Bank two . . . bank three . . . bank four . . . each gave me a no. Bank five . . . six . . . seven . . . eight also came and went much to my disappointment. Something was missing from the equation. I could feel it. I saw it in their faces as I laid out my track record and future plans. I could sense their reluctance to back my dream. Bank number nine liked the deal, but couldn't do it in time—another no. Banks 10 through 15 were a blur. One bank after another said no. What's wrong with these people? Or is it me?

I was determined from the very beginning. My conviction never wavered. In fact, it improved. And I steadily improved along with my chances of success. Every night that month, I walked around the block by my home, reciting a forceful 30-second soliloquy aimed at the faceless banker I would meet the next day. I sold myself on myself during this powerful speech. I began by stating my name, and continued speaking as if I was giving a 30-second commercial for a candidate running for political office. And that candidate was myself!

Even though I was alone in this situation I had my best friend— me—on my side. Bank 16 . . . 17 . . . two weeks until my financial deadline . . . bank 21 . . . 22 . . . 23 . . . My nightly talks grew more confident and motivational. I would change the belief and expectation of the banks I would see. I would change the belief and expectation about my club and its future as a solid loan for any institution. But first I had to change my belief and expectation.

On the 30th day, the last day, I visited my 42nd bank. And the loan officer said, "Absolutely yes." His staff swiftly prepared a bridge loan, and it bought some more time to finalize the deal that I envisioned 30 days earlier.

Unbeknownst to me, my wife had called Allied Van Lines to organize a possible move back to Ohio. With my home attached to the financing, it was possible for me to lose it all. Every time I see a moving van, I think of those times.

Thirty walks alone. Thirty "30-second commercials." Forty-one rejections. Thirty days. And one glorious yes. I remember that hot August years ago very well.

The 30-second commercial to you, for you, and by you works! Baseball all-stars, NBA veterans, tennis professionals, and the best golfers in the world have given this short monologue to themselves. Ironically, several bankers I have since coached used the tool to slay their own dragons.

If you desire to advance to the next level in your profession or sport, maybe all you need is a little more belief and expectancy. Try selling yourself on yourself.

Stand up alone in a quiet room or go for a long walk. With your posture erect and your chin placed high above your sternum, open your talk by stating your name. My name is . . . Speak your name with pride, and pronounce each syllable with clarity and conviction. Next, deal from strength. State in positive "I" statements the actions that you are taking to accomplish your mission. Say the words as if they're so. Feel the words and deliver them with passion. Use body language and gestures that are animated and convincing. Sell your ideas, beliefs, and expectations. Change your voice inflections, and occasionally pause for dramatic effect. Pepper your talk with adjectives of strength, power, and quality. Be convincing! Speak with authority. Last, close your commercial with a call to action. Finish with dominance and purpose.

In the spirit of the political conventions, maybe it's time to sell yourself on yourself. Good fortune favors the bold. Do it!

Can you have too much optimism? I've known many performers who believed they were so good that they didn't need to exercise the basics. They eventually entered into wishful thinking. Once this happens, a surprise from an opponent can send this performer crashing to defeat.

I spoke to a group of grocery-store managers in Chicago several years ago. The least-tenured person had been in the business 20 years. They were all so cocky. They had no interest in learning new tools. Even their dress habits reflected their laid-back "I'm untouchable" attitude. Their company recently was sold. Now only 2 of the 14 remain. The others were let out to pasture because they refused to change, refused to learn, and became overconfident. Now they are out of work.

Keep your O level in balance.

When champions and true champions are at their best, they have a high level of trust. They trust their preparedness. They trust their ability to adapt to stress. They trust their ability to adjust to changing conditions and circumstances. And most of all, they trust their "inner voice." You have intuitive thoughts on a daily basis. You've said before, "I have good vibes about him" or "I have bad vibes about my trip." Where did these vibes come from, and how did they reach your mind? Do you think they're coincidences? Do you act on them? Do you trust them?

The inner voice is your intuition or gut feeling for the situation. How many times have you answered a question on a test, only to replace it with another answer? You know the result. Wrong answer. Every time. How many times have you selected a seven iron in golf and before you strike the ball, your inner voice whispers, "Six iron?" What do you do? Do you use logic, or listen to your intuition? Your intuition possesses information that your conscious mind does not possess. Trust its power and wisdom. When you consistently listen to it, it will speak to you louder and more often. Ignore it, and it will whisper faintly. Dismiss it, and it will be as predictable as a rainbow.

Here's an example of trust: After receiving the S.C.O.R.E. System at one of my seminars, this financial adviser for Waddell & Reed Financial Services went out on the town. Alone. He had never gone to a nightclub before. He was shy and introverted. "I was not a ladies' man," he confided. His confidence from the seminar was soaring. He felt renewed. He trusted his instincts.

> *Your intuition possesses information that your conscious mind does not possess. Trust its power and wisdom. When you consistently listen to it, it will speak to you louder and more often.*

He was not trying to pick up women, mind you. He was following a vision of a kindred spirit who felt the same way he did. He was going to find a lady who would share his life. This was his first foray into the singles scene alone. After several hours, he had found no one who would dance with him or let him buy them a drink. Forty or more rebuffs and rejections had been thrown in his face. Yet he was not dejected. There was a purpose that drew him to this place. He had a vision. He had belief. He possessed expectancy.

Finally, as the evening wore on and the crowds began to thin, the man struck up a conversation with a stunning young woman. Talking to her was as easy as talking to his best friend. Two hours later, he left the place with her phone number carefully tucked into his wallet, and plans for a dinner date the very next evening.

Twelve years later, I was approached after a seminar by a man I did not recognize. He told me he had attended a seminar of mine over a decade before. He handed me something from his wallet and said, "This is the gift the System gave me." In my hands was a picture of two beautiful children. "Thank you," he said, with tears in his eyes. "Without the optimism the S.C.O.R.E. System instilled in me, without trusting my inner voice, I would never have met their mother on the last night of my seminar."

Optimism, or O, is the belief and expectancy that a task or group of tasks will lead to well-defined goals that lead to your vision.

How's your optimism level?

CHAPTER 6

Relaxation

"I'm soooo nervous. I'm freaking out." "I can't get this off my mind. I'm so worried." "I'm so tight. I'm afraid to make a mistake." These thoughts will produce negative actions and results. Sounds like these people need the next component of S.C.O.R.E. They need relaxation.

The Zone has been described as a "purposeful calm" and that calm is Relaxation, the fourth element of the S.C.O.R.E. chain. Most poor performances occur because we try too hard and force the action. We tense up during "moments of truth." We've all been nervous. We've all been tense before a performance. Most of us have experienced the feeling of the "butterflies." And we've all "frozen" at the wrong time and place.

Isn't it amazing how champions appear to perform effortlessly, as if they're not even trying? They breathe normally. Their jaw is unhinged, freeing the body to respond with lightning quickness and accuracy. They understand how their body responds to stress. They appear calm, smooth, and relaxed. They move through their arenas effortlessly. Mentally, champions are in harmony and at peace with the vision and their goals. And when they travel, they're calm and cool. It's as if they're in a vacuum. Nothing bothers them. Delays. Crowds. Obnoxious people. Unruly children. Overzealous fans. Nothing. They are unfazed.

OK, it's time to relax like a champion. Commit this definition to memory: *relaxation is being mentally and physically comfortable (free from worry or anxiety) with the task(s) to reach well-defined goals that lead to a vision.*

Relaxation is the state wherein you are less tense, rigid, strict, or severe. The high R performer is free from worry and anxiety, and especially free from the need to win at all costs.

The R is on the opposite side of self-discipline and concentration. When your S and C are too high, your relaxation will plummet. The champion, and especially the true champion, understands the need for balance in his life.

You now know that stress is the best friend of the champion. Champions create their own stress on their terms and timelines. Adapting to this stress is the art form. Programming your subconscious makes this happen. It activates the body to respond to stressful situations and conditions. First of all, stress, if not directed away from you, will hide in the muscles of your body. If you have an issue with a family member, a crisis at work, a personal weight problem, or not enough money in the bank, your subconscious will assist you in adapting to these situations. And it can perform this feat simultaneously. Behind the scenes, it begins pulling the strings for coincidence, luck, and opportunity. All for your benefit and gain.

However, if you are negative in dealing with this inner turmoil, the opposite will happen. This process will cause stress to hide in the body. Now stress becomes a negative energy force that literally resides in the muscles of the body. Once this occurs, your body will become constricted. You feel tight. You feel the tension of a body not free and loose. You will worry and become anxious. How do you know if you have low relaxation? Try this exercise:

EXERCISE #23

STRESS INVENTORY

There are many warning signs for negative stress. Most are unheeded. Beware of these signals warning of low R. They could be any of the following (if all are occurring simultaneously, put down the book as calmly as possible and have someone drive you immediately to your physician).

- *You can't hold your eyes still — they dart or twitch.*
- *Eye contact is difficult.*
- *Your hands perspire.*
- *You bite your fingernails.*
- *Your jaw is tense or locked.*
- *You grind your teeth.*
- *You bite your lips.*
- *You feel achy.*
- *You experience shortness of breath.*
- *Your voice cracks when you speak.*
- *You engage in excessive chatter.*
- *You have loss of energy and even sleep.*
- *Your stomach is in knots.*
- *You obsessively replay the past.*
- *You are always nauseous.*

- *You think the worst possible scenario as your first thought.*
- *You can't sleep through the night.*
- *You engage in imaginary role-playing (aggressive, combative, hostile, domineering) with a superior or authority figure.*
- *You put on the brakes or become tentative when confronted with a "moment of truth" situation.*
- *You're always concerned with what others think before a performance.*

These are all signals that your R Level is out of balance. Scour your mind and body for these warning signs. Heighten your awareness of negative stress symptoms.

The champion and the true champion are comfortable with their high but reachable goals. They are relaxed and calm during the execution of tasks. They are free of negative body language. They have peaceful thoughts. They have clarity, with less chaos, during a crisis. They are in control of their breathing. They breathe normally, especially when the intensity of the moment increases. The past is history. They learn from it and move on. Period! And they send their energy away from them toward targets and objectives.

In order to keep a balance while you pursue your vision, be sure to add times of mental and physical silence throughout your quarter, month, week, and day. When you are in the Zone, there is a rhythm not unlike the rhythm in music. In fact, music is *not* music without silence. Otherwise, it's just noise. Multiple sound tracks cause us to miss the silence. Add silence between the notes, and the music changes. Likewise, we need the silence of relaxation in our lives.

SHARPEN YOUR AX

Abraham Lincoln said, "If I had four hours to chop down a tree, I would spend two hours sharpening my ax." Have you been performing with a dull ax? Working hard, but going nowhere? We all need to rest. We all need to periodically renew our energy. Start with vacation time. Add it immediately upon preparing your year. You will have goals for the year, the quarter, the month, the week, and the day. Your R Level needs goals as well. Take as much time off as you can get. Most of us need vacations long before we take them. We are chopping the success tree with a dull ax.

Take daily breaks or minivacations. Break your day into quarters. Take a break at midmorning, at lunchtime and in the afternoon. Walk away from your work, then return refreshed and balanced. In addition, I recommended a massage once a week if you can afford it. Your body definitely will welcome this investment. Of the 19 major-league baseball all-stars I've coached, all of them received massages weekly, with most getting them daily. And 17 took naps every day, power naps of 10-20 minutes. In fact, Carlos Delgado hit four home runs with the Toronto Blue Jays in one game after he had a 30-minute power nap just before game time.

Here is a list of activities to sharpen your ax. Add more activities as you see fit.

- *Vacation*
- *"Ferris Bueller" day off (nothing planned)*
- *Nap*
- *Massage*
- *Taking a bath instead of a shower (bubbles, candles, wine optional)*
- *Whirlpool/sauna/steam room*
- *Dining alone (taking time to savor your meal)*
- *Yoga*

- *Morning and afternoon break (15 minutes)*
- *Music (anywhere and everywhere)*
- *Going to movies/plays/concerts*
- *Reading a good book*
- *Going for a walk*
- *Hobby*
- *Performing music (sing, dance, or play)*
- *Weekend getaway*
- *Leaving work early*
- *Sleeping late on weekends*
- *Exercising*
- *Meditating*
- *Monthly "Silence Day"*
- *Martial arts*

Yes, your brain needs silent moments. Try this.

EXERCISE #25

MONTHLY "SILENCE DAY"

Once a month, conduct a personal "Silence Day." On this day, speak only at a minimum. Quiet your mind. Avoid past and future thoughts. Engage in the moment. Listening is your main activity. When you feel like judging or offering your opinion, pass. You'll know when to employ this day. Most are a few days too late. Add a Silence Day to your calendar.

How do you increase your R before or during a performance?

You may feel nervous. You may be tense. You may experience the butterflies. Butterflies? Do you know what causes them? Do you know they're *good* for you? When an upcoming event is very important to you, your body will adjust just before it begins. Your body will prepare to combat any problems or obstacles. The blood vessels and capillaries in the stomach instantly constrict. Next, the blood is diverted to the brain for clarity. Then it travels to the large muscles for inordinate strength, balance, quickness, and agility. The constriction in the stomach will give you the feeling of the butterflies. Are you nervous? No. It is at this moment that your body is preparing to attract the Zone.

If your awareness is one of "I'm so nervous," or I'm freaking out," the energy in your body will lodge in your muscles, causing referral constriction everywhere. If this tension occurs and begins to alter your thinking, try one of these techniques before your overall performance level drops.

EXERCISE #26

STICK YOUR TONGUE OUT

You cannot be in a Zone mind-set without your jaw being unhinged. In fact, this is why Michael Jordan stuck his tongue out when he went to the basket for a dunk. When Kobe Bryant hit his game-tying three-pointer that enabled the Los Angeles Lakers to win game two against the Detroit Pistons in the 2004 NBA Finals, his jaw was unhinged and his tongue was out of his mouth at the moment of the release of his shot. Now, those of us in business can't walk around with our tongues hanging out. But we can have a consciousness, an awareness, of our jaw muscles. When the jaw, and consequently the rest of the body, are relaxed, your muscles become the positive slaves to the blueprint of your performance that is locked in your mind. Being relaxed while putting a golf ball or giving a speech or sales presentation will ensure a solid performance. Muhammad Ali fought with his jaw unhinged. That's why he lost his mouth guard during his fights. In fact, this is why he got his jaw broken in a heavyweight world championship fight against Ken Norton.

Periodically, scour your body for tension or negative stress. Check your jaw. Are you grinding your teeth? Are you holding your breath while you're performing? Check your jaw when you're driving in rush-hour traffic. Check for low relaxation before and during any performance where you desire to be your best. So the next time you face a 10-foot putt for the club championship, unhinge your jaw, breathe normally, and stick out your tongue like Jordan.

Let's move on to our next exercise to elevate your relaxation level.

EXERCISE #27

BREATHE LIKE A BABY

Babies can get into a deep sleep quickly. Here is how they relax so fast. Begin by inhaling deeply. Unhinge your jaw. Place all of your awareness on your breathing. Feel your lungs fill with positive, energized air. Now exhale negative, stale air. Place your left hand on your stomach. With every inhale and exhale, let your stomach move your hand. Breathe through your stomach. Be aware of your hand being moved. After a few deep breaths, you'll start to feel your shoulders relax. Slowly, repeat inhaling and exhaling, until you are in a relaxed rhythm. Within 30 seconds you will feel more relaxed. Use this technique anytime and anywhere.

Try this next exercise before bedtime for a better night's sleep.

EXERCISE #28

TENSION RELEASE

By constricting the muscles in your body you will also constrict the blood flow to the area of tightness. When you release or relax the mus-

cles, blood flows back to this area. This tension-release exercise will rid the area of undue stress.

Tighten your facial muscles by scrunching your face as if you're straining to lift a heavy weight. Hold this tension for five seconds. Be careful not to overtax yourself. When you relax . . . exhale . . . then feel the tingle of the blood flowing back to your face. You can tense the following muscle groups in sequence or isolation: face, jaw, shrug shoulders to neck, hands, biceps, upper and lower abdominal group, buttocks, hamstrings, thighs, calves, and feet.

Use tension release for a quick fix during a performance or for inducing a drowsy, alpha state-of-mind for visualization or as an aid for getting to sleep.

Here's a tool that will assist you when confronted with adversity. This requires practice but it's worth it.

EXERCISE #29

THE PALM TREE

Our thoughts and feelings flow continuously in an unending stream— our consciousness is always switched on, with the exception of deep

sleep cycles. We act on these thoughts and feelings in some way every moment. But how often do we pay attention to our inner life and its manifestations in our body language and reactions—and their effects on others? For example, do you ever get angry? Anger is never the first emotion. Feelings of frustration, jealousy, impatience, or embarrassment can occur without your conscious acknowledgment long before you lose your temper. I encourage you to be mindful of your thoughts and emotions and how they lead to negative actions.

True champions develop this mindfulness of their inner life. In the next few days, be aware of your true thoughts and feelings. Try this the next time you are in a situation that could lead to anger. As soon as a circumstance, condition, or event displeases you or disturbs you, think of the palm tree. Have a palm-tree thought before that hurricane reaches full force.

The palm tree reacts to a hurricane or violent storm by allowing the negativity to pass through it by bending with the wind. It absorbs the wrath of the devastating winds. After the storm dissipates and leaves, the palm stands up straight to see another day of sunshine. It symbolizes all that's good about the sun, the beach, the ocean, recreation, and pleasure.

So the next time you are confronted by an angry driver on the road or a loved one who is blowing off steam, be the palm tree!

EXERCISE #30

THE OAK TREE

An oak tree, of course, would brace itself and fight 80 to 100 mph winds. It would fight with all of its strength to not succumb to hurricane force. With a mighty but futile attempt, it would be left with shattered branches or a broken trunk. Maybe it would be uprooted and scattered. However, if the situation presents itself, you may need to stand tall like the mighty oak. At first, be silent. Then, if the problem is still there and *you see the palm-tree approach will not work, you can just say. "This is not acceptable!" And then say nothing else. Whoever talks next will lose. Sometimes you need to stand your ground and be the oak tree. You'll feel like the mighty oak after you wield this tool. And not using it appropriately, well . . . this is not acceptable!*

Are you a palm tree or an oak tree in the face of adversity? Keep both of these images in your mind. Be prepared when the time comes to employ their power. If you are not sure what to do, by all means say and do *nothing*. Be aware of your thoughts and feelings, and you will control your actions and ultimately your results.

How do you overcome worry and anxiety?

Worry occurs when you anchor your thoughts into the past, replaying the same scene over and over in your mind. Then you magnify this thought and feeling and project it into the future by using your imagination, usually creating a scenario that will never occur. These negative images keep the energy in your body, and the muscles take the hit. It can paralyze you. Catch yourself when you mentally replay a past situation. Learn from it and go on. Replaying the negative past has no positive effect on the future. If these replays continue, turn your brain off or divert your thoughts to something else. My recommendation is to think about your positive vision.

How do you relax when faced with a "moment of truth" situation?

Champions handle these pivotal moments in a performance by only executing the basics of their craft. They are ok with just reaching their standard during these times. A standard is a minimum requirement for a satisfactory performance. Of course, a champion wants to perform to her maximum. By mentally establishing an easier-to-achieve minimum, she reduces the stress and tension that get in the way of flow and performance. This is the champion's secret: take the pressure off, don't try too hard. The results are amazing.

By learning the discipline of relaxation, we don't have to work as hard to stay in the Zone, where we accomplish the tasks set out before us to achieve our vision.

How's your relaxation level?

CHAPTER 7

Enjoyment

L ast is the dessert. It's a laugh, giggle, snicker, belly laugh, smile, or grin. It's passion, satisfaction, pleasure, excitement, enthusiasm, happiness, exuberance, and joy. Enjoyment is the absolute end of the acronym S.C.O.R.E. and the end product of S.C.O.R.E. System.

Commit this definition to memory: *enjoyment is the satisfaction and/or pleasure of executing the task(s) to reach well-defined goals that lead to a vision.*

Enjoyment reflects your passion, enthusiasm, excitement, joy, exuberance, happiness, and zest for living. Having these thoughts and feelings will give you a look and demeanor that is coveted by friends, families, employers, and coworkers everywhere.

Enjoyment is your passion and enthusiasm for doing what you do. If you don't enjoy it, then what's the point? How many people do you know who hate their jobs? You can see it on their faces. You can hear it in their words and see it in their deeds. How many people do you know who complain about their lives? We see many low E people in the world. They talk, feel, and act like they're in a rut. Most can't get out of it. They plod along day to day totally stagnant. The days turn into weeks, months, and years. Entire blocks of a person's life can fly by with little or no enthusiasm for living. It's all work and no play.

Champions love what they do. Olympic champion Dan O'Brien told me, "I love to practice. I absolutely love my training regimen. And most of all, I love the thrill of competition." The peak performer even possesses enjoyment and enthusiasm when confronted with problems and obstacles. He had a passion for problem solving. That's right! For true champions, all problems are opportunities. People love to see other people in problematic situations. We love watching others having confrontations. "How will they respond? How will they handle this?" Most of us would rather avoid these situations. Not the true champions. You've seen them perform under stressful conditions. They relish these moments. Their enjoyment is contagious. When they walk into the arena, the entire crowd feels their energy. It's this ingredient that makes an individual an MVP in any group or organization.

Performing at a high level *without* enjoyment will eventually have disastrous results. Likewise, getting the fun, laughter, and passion back into your life will place you on the true champion's pathway. Here's an example of enjoyment and the power of laughter.

As I mentioned earlier, I was coaching Adriano Panatta, Italy's number one tennis player and top ranked in the world. He was a champion, but not in the following conditions and circumstances.

The tournament schedule dictated we travel to the grass courts of England to prepare for Wimbledon, the ultimate test of a tennis player. All young tennis players dream about performing on those hallowed grounds. All except my guy. He hated grass courts. He said, "I'm a clay-court specialist. I'm a dirt player. Come on, grass is for cows." This is how we traveled to England. His enjoyment level was low before we hit British soil. He said, "I know I'm playing this warm-up tournament tomorrow, but if I lose I'd like to go back to Rome." I said, "Are you nuts? Lose? Back to Rome! Wimbledon starts in less than 10 days. Come on, let's focus. Let's lock in mentally."

During his opening match, he turned to me in the stands and yelled, "I told you, grass is for cows." I cringed at the scrutiny of the other spectators. And he proceeded to lose easily. No passion. No desire. No fun. With Wimbledon next, he left England for Rome to see his family. "Jim, I promise I'll be back in a few days." And he left. I was alone in London, thinking to myself, "What am I doing here?" The very next day, Heathrow airport shut down due to an airline strike. No flights could come in from Rome. For over a week, I was alone in London. No Panatta. No practice. No enjoyment.

Finally, two nights before the first round of Wimbledon, he returned. I had one day to help him get ready on a surface that he didn't like. Talk about low enjoyment. To make matters worse, it started to rain. The outdoor courts were flooded. Oh, that was great!

Luckily, I found an indoor synthetic grass court about an hour and a half outside of London. As we drove there (on the wrong side of the road), I started laughing at how ridiculous this situation was. Here we were at the Big W, and we didn't practice until the day before! It was comical. It was now the biggest joke. We both started laughing at the situation. I had tears running down my face, and so did he. This was probably the first time he had laughed in some time. He played Guillermo Villas (the world's number one player) in practice, and he beat him like a drum. He played loose and relaxed. He was laughing.

If he missed a shot, he laughed. He laughed through two sets of incredible tennis.

Wimbledon began the next day. We didn't even warm up. Ha-ha-ha. And he laughed through the first round victoriously. He laughed through the second round. No practice. Adriano Panatta got his E level up through laughing at the situation. We laughed all the way to the quarterfinals of the biggest tennis tournament in the world. Not bad for a player that never won a match on a grass court. Sometimes you just need to laugh and detach from the possible outcome of the performance.

Now check your laugh-o-meter with the following exercise.

EXERCISE #31

LAUGH INVENTORY

Take out your life arenas and mentally peruse each for the quantity and quality of laughter. Which arena contains the most laughter? Which one has the least? Which arena do you need to increase your own laughter? Which person is the sourpuss?

Write down the names of five people in your life that need to laugh more. Your assignment is to increase their laughter. Maybe you need to start with a smile, and then work your way up from there. You be the judge. Take your own laughter inventory, as well as those of the people around you.

Next is the power of music. Make it a vital part of your life. I've had the same heart song for the last decade. It plays in my mind before every seminar I conduct. I truly believe that music is a direct pipeline to getting in the Zone. The reason that music is so important to people's lives is the rhythmic beat that causes people to start tapping their toes, bobbing their heads, and getting into the groove—just feeling the rhythm of the sounds. We like that as human beings. It's enjoyable.

And it doesn't matter what kind of music — it could be rap or classical. All music has a beat.

I've coached athletes who have had a song in their mind as they walked into the arena. They kept that song in their head and played the best they ever played. That's because the music gave them a rhythmical feeling of enjoyment that helped them attract the zone.

EXERCISE #32

A SONG IN YOUR HEART

Your exercise is to find your heart song. It's the one song that puts pep in your step and joy back in your soul. Next time, when you find yourself not enjoying a moment, think of your heart song. I want you to hear it and, most important, feel it. Sometimes people even whistle to their heart-song. Many of the athletes I've coached use their heart song as a sound track for all of their mental dress rehearsals. It plays in the background to their life movie.

Yes, I use this *next* exercise personally. Go ahead. Snicker. But when you've employed it, I promise that you'll smile, laugh, and feel better. It may take a little courage, especially when others are present. But I promise it works. Cross my heart. Promise.

EXERCISE #33

SKIP

Can you imagine a 305-pound Chicago Bears lineman skipping on and off the field in a game on national television? After coaching Evan Pilgrim for three months, he finally started for the Bears. In front of a sellout crowd at Soldier Field, he was called for an offside penalty and a holding penalty in one series of downs. His coach was infuriated. When he came off the field, he was berated. It wasn't a pretty sight to see. On the next series, I watched him skip onto the field, much to the chagrin of the coach. I'll admit I was initially stunned. From the stands, I watched this huge man skip onto the gridiron, and I smiled. On the first play, he flattened the man in front of him and proceeded downfield to throw another enormous block that helped the Bears score a touchdown. Wow! Sometimes you just need to skip.

Now, I want you to skip. That's right. Skip. You cannot be in a bad mood when skipping. Skipping will change your mood almost instantly. You might see my clients skip to the mound or skip down the fairway. Try it. You'll see what I mean.

This next exercise will make some people feel guilty. But not the champion!

EXERCISE #34

TREAT YOURSELF

When I asked two billionaires what made them great, both said, "I reward myself for a job well done." What if you don't reach the goal? You could reward yourself anyway. "I don't," replied both wealthy men. Create a short- and long-term reward system for your best friend—you. Make a list of all your arena goals and their deadlines. Next to each place a reward that you and/or your team will receive: a massage, a new car, jewelry, a weekend getaway, a spa treatment, an upgrade to a suite on your next trip, a day off, first-class airfare . . . you decide. Now you can use the dynamic technique of aftermath visualization.

See in your mind your goal being attained. See it as if it's so. Now see yourself taking possession of your reward. See it and feel the enjoyment from a job well done.

Enjoyment is last but not least in the S.C.O.R.E. chain. It has the power to make you truly happy. But what is happiness? Over the last three decades, I've known many happy people. They get it. Here's my prescription for happiness.

- Look at problems as challenges and opportunities.
- Spend the majority of your waking hours in the now.
- Be truly thankful every day—not just on Thanksgiving, Christmas, or birthdays.
- Wake up happy and go to bed happy.
- Greet everyone with a smile and a positive outlook.
- Say good-bye to people as if you had been truly glad to see them.
- Feel you are an integral part of the whole—not just in your business or your family, but in the human race. Feel like you can make a difference by living.
- Treat the elderly with reverence and respect, and children with passion and joy.
- Go into the future for planning and into the past *only* for evaluating and learning.
- *Do not* judge or act like a victim.
- Talk to yourself as a *best friend*.
- Think less and produce more.
- Exercise the Golden Rule: Do unto others as you would have them do unto you. (This is not limited to the religious.)
- Give more than you receive.
- Manage your thoughts on a daily basis. Happy people think about what they think about.
- Manage your personal energy.
- Smile and laugh a lot.
- Have music in your heart and life.
- *Do not* get bothered by small issues.
- Move physically with high energy.

- Adjust to changing conditions and circumstances.
- Manage all five components of S.C.O.R.E.
- Use the 90-second and 5-second rules.
- Possess simplicity and balance in all life arenas.

Enjoyment is the satisfaction and/or pleasure derived from executing the task or group of tasks that leads to your goals and ultimately your vision.

How's your enjoyment level?

CHAPTER 8

S.C.O.R.E. Levels

Now you know the pieces of the S.C.O.R.E. System. Together they form a delicate chain that unlocks your mental and physical potential. These intangibles are mutually dependent. This domino-like chain is only as strong as its weakest link. You are responsible for all repairs and must keep the chain intact and balanced as you move in and out of each life arena.

Which part of S.C.O.R.E. needs your attention most? Does this answer change when you change arenas? In your Business Arena, you may need more optimism. Yet in your Family Arena, you may need more self-discipline. And in your Golf Arena, you may need relaxation, especially when the money is on the table. Of course, next week all of these scenarios may be different according to shifting conditions and circumstances.

When bound together, each component of S.C.O.R.E. forms your overall attitude, or S.C.O.R.E. Level. These five intangibles move as a unit from high to low attitude and vice versa. When S.C.O.R.E. is balanced, it moves toward the Zone. When it is out of balance with either too much or too little self-discipline, concentration, optimism, relaxation, or enjoyment, it will plummet toward a depressed state of mind I call the Downs. Your S.C.O.R.E. Level can rise and fall with lightning speed.

One of my first major experiences with the swiftness of this mind-set change occurred in Columbus, Ohio, in the early 1970s. It happened while playing an exhibition tennis match against my childhood idol—the great Pancho Gonzalez.

Facing this legendary tennis player was a dream come true, and I was excited to be playing him while he was still a world-class player. As the match began, I had so much energy inside of me that everything seemed in slow motion—I was locked in the moment. The first time I served, I hit an ace. I won the second point with another ace. I was in the Zone, and Pancho knew immediately. He felt my presence, and he was caught off guard.

Leading 4–1 in the first set, I sat down at the changeover while Pancho grabbed the microphone from the umpire and said to me for everyone in the crowd to hear, "You're unbelievable. I've never seen anyone so good. Where are you from?" Like a fool, I replied, "Kentucky." And then Pancho said, "You know, I'm one of the best players in the world, and I've never lost to a boy from Kentucky." Everybody started to laugh, and for the first time in the match, so did I—nervously.

He gave the microphone back to the umpire, and I sat in my chair and thought, "Oh my gosh, I'm playing one of the best players in the world—Pancho Gonzalez." Exit my discipline level. I started thinking about what happened and what could happen. As the next game began, my energy was not being sent freely to my targets—no, I started thinking about me and what I needed to do. Exit concentration.

My optimism level was very high before the match began. But suddenly I was playing my childhood idol. I remember holding my throat—the classic universal signal for choking. Good-bye optimism.

I became so tight. I could barely breathe. Relaxation was gone. Suddenly, this was not fun anymore, and with that my enjoyment evaporated.

The next thing I remember was sitting in the locker room with my head slumped on the tail end of a 6–4, 6–1 defeat. As I looked up I saw Pancho preening in the mirror. He came over and patted me on the head and said, "Kid, you just need some experience. You need more confidence." And I never saw him again.

Isn't it amazing how one moment you're in the Zone and the next minute you're in the Downs?

We've all experienced these sudden attitude changes in ourselves, our family members, and our coworkers. For example, say you're having a great dinner with your spouse or significant other and one of you brings up a sore subject from the past. Just like that, the mood of the moment turns upside down. Negative body language, sarcasm, and eventually silence invade the peacefulness of a great night out. Our S.C.O.R.E. Levels are vulnerable to the blinding ambush of a dirty look, a misguided word, or a negative future- or past-tense thought.

> *Everyone has a S.C.O.R.E. Level, regardless of age, ethnic background, religion, sex, social status, or experience.*

Understanding how this happens will unlock your ability to perform at your highest level as a coach or active participant in any arena.

The S.C.O.R.E. chain moves as a unit through five possible performance levels. You can enter and exit these levels many times during a day.

THE ZONE
HIGH S.C.O.R.E.
S.C.O.R.E.
LOW S.C.O.R.E.
THE DOWNS

Managing the balance of S.C.O.R.E. is the key to being successful and performing like a true champion. The difficulty lies in the fact that S.C.O.R.E. Levels *will* fluctuate. Your S.C.O.R.E. Level can oscillate dramatically up and down 30 to 40 times during the course of a day. From the Zone to the Downs and back again, a performer can have a roller-coaster day. A dirty look, a misunderstanding, bad weather, or criticism from a superior can instantaneously turn someone who was in the Zone into someone now in the "Downs."

The Zone

Now you know that to attract this peak mind-set, you need equally high levels of self-discipline, concentration, optimism, relaxation, and enjoyment. I've witnessed athletes, executives, teams, and companies locked in the Zone for approximately 30 days. This

When you're aware of being in the Zone, you're not in it.

is where records are broken and goals are surpassed. You can expend tremendous energy when staying in the Zone for this duration. Many of us do not possess the emotional endurance to sustain this mental pace. Recovery from this mind-body fusion can take a good deal of time. The more you perform in the Zone, the greater your capacity for staying there and returning there.

High S.C.O.R.E.

This mind-set is the same as the Zone with one major difference. It's easily disturbed. High S.C.O.R.E. is the Zone at its most fragile state. You make an eight-foot birdie putt and get excited—and just like that, your next tee shot is in the woods. You are locked into a great book, immersed in the emotion of the characters, and someone interrupts your reading. Poof! Just like that, you can't find the images and feelings of the characters on the page. You lose your focus and put the book down.

High S.C.O.R.E. lasts a minimum of approximately 12 seconds. Champions move in and out of this S.C.O.R.E. Level many times during the day, usually in their work arena. True champions get in High S.C.O.R.E. as they enter every arena.

S.C.O.R.E.

This is your baseline attitude. You may favor the high or the low end of the spectrum. How you were raised as a child has to do with your typical daily mind-set. Which parent had the highest and lowest S.C.O.R.E. Level? Mom or Dad? Which parent do you favor? Your current environment can also have a lot to do with your base mind-set. If your work is not enjoyable, your overall S.C.O.R.E. Level could be low. If your relationship with your spouse or significant others is in harmony, your S.C.O.R.E. Level will reflect it.

Low S.C.O.R.E.

, five basic states of mind, this is the *most* important. Surprised? ͵s is where we begin to see symptoms of hitting the bottom—of get- ͵ng an "attitudinal flu." When we get the attitudinal sniffles, they need to be nursed with immediate first aid. Recognizing these verbal and nonverbal cues is the key to thinking like a champion. Here is a short list of the keys to Low S.C.O.R.E.

Low Self-discipline

- No goals are set.
- Every day is generalized.
- Emotions cloud reason.
- Mistake tolerance is low.
- Your rhythm is dominated by external factors.
- Your movements are excessive and complicated.
- You have a tendency to procrastinate.
- You have a tendency to rush or hurry.
- Your life arenas are complicated and overlapping.
- Routines are haphazard or nonexistent.
- You feel lost and disorganized.
- You have a tendency to quit or give up.

Low Concentration

- Tasks are not completed.
- There are too many tasks.
- You are easily distracted.
- Tasks are not clearly defined.
- Future-tense thoughts occur.
- Past-tense thoughts occur.
- Time is out of control.
- Eyes wander and generalize.

Low Optimism

- You have no energy in your voice and/or body movement.
- Your posture is slumping.
- You avoid eye contact.
- Verbal negatives abound.
- You feel little or no sense of worth.
- You don't feel loved or cherished.
- You are unsure about goals, strategies, and/or tactics.
- You have little pride.
- You feel envy.
- You feel guilty when you indulge in a selfish activity.
- Your negative past follows you.
- Wishful thinking enters your mind.
- Daily habits are negative (dress, eating, hygiene).
- You question your abilities and talents.
- You place too much emphasis on what others think.

Low Relaxation

- You're uncomfortable with goals, strategies, and tactics.
- You worry because of the past.
- You are anxious over the future.
- You have a loss of energy.
- You feel panic and/or desperation.
- You feel fatigued.
- Your body is sending you negative cues.
    - o Twitching, darting, or blinking eyes
    - o Perspiring hands
    - o Wringing of the hands
    - o Excessive hand placement on the throat area
    - o Biting fingernails, lip, or inner mouth
    - o Tense shoulders
    - o Jerky or excessive movements

o Dry mouth

o Excessive yawning

o Tight chest

o Grinding teeth

o Tense jaw

o Shortness of breath

o Cracked voice

o Excessive chatter

Low Enjoyment

- You lack enthusiasm.
- There is a low energy level in voice.
- The E level of your environment alters your own.
- You make sarcastic, snippy, and curt remarks.
- You're apathetic concerning goals and tasks.
- You're easily bored.
- You have little or no body animation.
- You're void of hand gestures and smiles.
- Your eyes lack sparkle and brightness.
- You're coasting or going through the motions.
- You have little or no desire.
- You verbally and nonverbally approach tasks with dread.
- You're too self-disciplined.
- You're never satisfied.
- You're trying too hard.
- You're forcing the action from despair.
- You desire the contest, event, or activity to end.

Negative talk and de-energized body language are easy reads for most of us. However, the great teachers can read the smallest signals of low S.C.O.R.E. in their pupils. They recognize learning is inhibited unless their students are in High S.C.O.R.E. or the Zone. Likewise, the great salesperson knows the buying process is blocked when the prospect has low levels of any S.C.O.R.E. component.

Remember: balance your S.C.O.R.E. Level, and your performance level rises. If there is an imbalance in your S.C.O.R.E., your performance level will plummet.

Here are some examples.

When your self-discipline is too high, your enjoyment will eventually drop.

ALL WORK AND NO PLAY

Likewise, when your enjoyment rises ("Let's party!"), your self-discipline will drop.

ALL PLAY AND NO WORK

Now you're being cocky.

OVERCONFIDENT; WISHFUL THINKING

Balance and simplicity are the keys for the Zone.

HIGH S.C.O.R.E./ZONE PERFORMANCE

The Downs

When you plummet into the Downs mind-set, you've entered a mild or severe depression. You have bypassed all symptoms with little or no remedies applied. Most of the time, Low S.C.O.R.E. was never recognized. Now you've entered an attitudinal quagmire that has characteristics of despair, hopelessness, frustration, worry, and anxiety. Many performers quit or give up when in the Downs. The judge and the victim in us rear their ugly heads. You may feel sad or empty, and others have noticed that you appear sad, tearful, and without joy. Sarcasm thrives. You may experience a significant loss of pleasure in either all or almost all of your daily activities. Your E level is very low. You may feel extreme fatigue or loss of energy. You may have difficulty falling asleep, or you may want to sleep too much. Your C level will fluctuate wildly, and you can experience difficulty in memory or focusing on one thing at a time. This mind-set can be highly contagious. Yes, misery loves company.

When experiencing the Downs mind-set, many people may need to see a physician if several symptoms last for at least two weeks in a row. Others may need to bottom out in order to rebound to High S.C.O.R.E. and the Zone. Remember, we are at our best as humans when things are at their worst. The negative stress of the Downs can automatically catapult us to a Zone state. However, the Downs can last hours, days, weeks, and even months. Avoiding the Downs is crucial. Too much damage can be done in any arena. Having the Downs will crash the growth in any life arena as apathy blankets opportunity as if smothering a fire. This is why reading Low S.C.O.R.E. symptoms is mandatory in reaching peak performance. When the individual elements of S.C.O.R.E. show signs of plummeting, repairs must take place to prevent the Downs. When self-discipline drops, concentration will follow suit. Soon, optimism will wane, and this can affect your ability to stay relaxed. Enjoyment will shortly join the rest at the bottom of the barrel.

When you are observing individuals and groups, be aware of the *physical, emotional,* and *intuitive* cues that are being broadcast. These three reactions (individually and accumulatively) from each person's thoughts will reveal their high or low S.C.O.R.E.

By reading others' S.C.O.R.E. Levels, you will improve the speed and ability at which you learn. Recognizing low optimism will arm the salesperson in motivating buyers to purchase. Recognizing low relaxation in your prospects may be telling you to back off from your pressure tactics. Reading S.C.O.R.E. Levels will increase your ability to parent, and it will help you forge relationships that can last a lifetime. Most of all, it will keep you on track in attaining your personal dreams.

It's not enough to just say that someone has a bad attitude. What is the cause? Which component of S.C.O.R.E. is the weakest link? What strategies and tactics you take as a teacher, a manager, a parent, or a coach depends on your S.C.O.R.E. reading? Remember, all thoughts have three reactions: physical, emotional, and intuitive. With the "tells" from these reactions, you can ascertain what each person is thinking. Now you will know exactly how to assist him in raising his performance. You will be able to read the thoughts of your students, customers, family members, and coworkers, as well as yourself. Understanding the five components of S.C.O.R.E. is just the beginning. Understanding how the components work in harmony will unleash the awareness necessary to change families, teams, companies, and communities. It is that powerful. Period.

READ ME LIKE A BOOK

⌐ irt reading the S.C.O.R.E. Level of people you meet or observe. Your next assignment is to recognize Low S.C.O.R.E. symptoms in the next arena you enter. Acknowledge Low S.C.O.R.E. and swiftly find the weakest link. Read the optimism level in your spouse. Notice that he doesn't smile or has low energy in his voice. Read your kids by noticing their discipline level or their lack of concentration. See the low relaxation in your immediate superior. Find the telltale signs of Low S.C.O.R.E. By reading others, you will more readily recognize your own symptoms that prevent you from performing in the Zone.

S.C.O.R.E. TRACKER

This exercise will reveal the needed area of growth for each team member and consequently the weak link for the entire team. Rate the S.C.O.R.E. level of each person in your company, department, athletic team, or family on a 1 to 10 scale (10 is the highest). Use the following model for a 10 rating.

S- This person has goals and is committed to achieving them. He is patient and under control of the situation. He is punctual and ready to perform immediately. He has strategies and tactics and is prepared to alter them if necessary.

C- This person has high quality in their work or play. She is accurate. She performs with little distraction. She only needs to be told once when given direction. She completes each task before moving on to the next.

O- *This person is confident and looks confident. He is always upbeat and looks for solutions instead of dwelling on problems. His verbal and nonverbal language is positive.*

R- *This person is calm and cool under pressure. She does not worry or express anxiety. Her jaw is unhinged as she performs, and she breathes normally.*

E- *This person is a delight to be around. He laughs and exudes enthusiasm and excitement. When he performs, you can feel his passion for the activity.*

Now write down the names of the individuals that you would like to rate from a group. Under each letter of S.C.O.R.E. rate each person on a 1 to 10 scale.

For Example:

Name	S	C	O	R	E
J. Smith	8	7	9	4	5
S. Jones	7	8	8	5	6
T. Lowe	4	5	7	6	7
F. Byers	8	8	8	8	7
J. Johns	7	7	8	5	4
A. Doe	8	8	8	6	6
Total:	42	43	48	(34)	(35)

Now you can tell the perceived weak link in each person, and you can also ascertain the overall weak link of the group. The above group has a low relaxation and enjoyment level. Using this information, a coach in this arena can create an atmosphere to balance the S.C.O.R.E. Level of the whole.

CHAPTER 9

Why Do S.C.O.R.E. Levels Fluctuate?

Change is an absolute. And your S.C.O.R.E. Level is no different. It *will* fluctuate. Can you manage the mental roller coaster of highs and lows? Do you plummet to Low S.C.O.R.E. when confronted with a reckless, uncaring driver? Did an obscene gesture cause you to think and even act in an aggressive manner? How about when you're waiting in line as a lazy, apathetic bank teller plods her way through the day's work? Do you look at your watch as your chest tightens from your frustration and impatience? Do you blow your breath and mumble about the slow service to anyone that will listen? Is the teller's ineptitude allowed to alter your S.C.O.R.E.?

Do you sometimes feel that you're not in control of your

S.C.O.R.E. Level? Is there someone in your life that seems to be pulling the strings of your S.C.O.R.E. like a puppeteer? That person's mood dictates your mood. And many times you walk on eggshells when they're in a bad frame of mind. How about when you are in High S.C.O.R.E. and the people around are *not*. They are indifferent. They don't share your positive thoughts or feelings. Who wins? Do you succumb to grumpy-itis? Or do you change their S.C.O.R.E. Level from Low to High?

Your S.C.O.R.E. may have 40 to 50 daily fluctuations. That's ok. However, keeping the wild swings from the Zone to the Downs and back again is your quest. Having Low S.C.O.R.E. moments is ok as long as you read them swiftly . . . and then balance the weak link . . . and then move on. Once you are aware of the high and low swings you will be on your way to preventing them. Champions avoid the pot-holes of Low S.C.O.R.E. — but if they do land in one, they recover swiftly with the precision of an Indy driver.

As you move from arena to arena, you'll encounter many factors that can raise or lower your S.C.O.R.E. Level and consequently attract or repel the Zone. These factors are the external and internal stimuli called S.C.O.R.E. Makers and Breakers.

S.C.O.R.E. Breakers wreak havoc with nonchampions. And they are a constant menace and threat to the champion. They can ambush you before you get to work or return home. A phone call saying a loved one is gravely sick can alter your S.C.O.R.E. Level before you walk in the door. An angry boss can deflate your O level and threaten your job just as you exit the workplace for home. After you enter an arena, a Breaker can penetrate your mind like a thief in the night. It can double or triple your thoughts in an instant. From the past to the future and back again, the Breaker can ricochet negatives throughout your mind like a pinball machine. The last quarter's negative financial statement finally arrives on your desk, sending your S.C.O.R.E. Level crashing to the Downs. Breakers can alter a performance with lightning speed. Are you immunized from their destructive power?

Does the negative body language of others pull you down? Do you let other people's words walk into your mind like intruders? Have you shielded yourself from the negatives of bad weather, less-than-desirable conditions, and/or pressurized circumstances? Are you guarded against the highs and lows of your own expectations? Has love blinded you to the rest of your life arenas? Has the thought of sex taken over the controls of your body like an alien from a sci-fi B movie? Remember: You have free will. How you think and consequently how you feel and act are choices that you and only you can make.

Let's look at the external and internal stimuli that can cause these mild or severe S.C.O.R.E. fluctuations. After your review of

> *S.C.O.R.E. Breakers can side-track the disciplined and penetrate the heaviest armor of confidence and positive self-esteem. They can tense up the coolest, most relaxed performer. And they can drop your enjoyment the way night drops the temperature in the desert; and they can shrink your enjoyment instantly.*

the broad categories, catalog your Makers and Breakers within your own arenas and personal experiences. Know the potential S.C.O.R.E. Breakers before you enter your next arena as a player or a coach. Immunize yourself against all potential negative influences.

The following lists provide examples of S.C.O.R.E. Makers and Breakers. These are referenced as external or internal. External Makers and Breakers can be anything we can see, touch, hear, taste, and smell. Internal Makers and Breakers are intangibles that occur only inside your body and mind, such as love, hate, sexual desire, and the anticaption of future events and the memory of past events. Look over this list. See what pertains to you.

Positive or Negative **External** *Stimuli*

- **Language.** A kind word or a hateful tone can alter S.C.O.R.E.
  - o Criticism, especially from a loved one, can tear up a S.C.O.R.E. Level like a shredder. When delivered with malice, it can make you cross your arms in defense then tighten your throat like a hangman's noose. As we gather our thoughts, we retaliate with venomous barbs aimed to penetrate love and friendship like shrapnel from a grenade. Even constructive criticism has everyone holding their breath in anticipation of a defensive outburst.
  - o Gossip is another potential Breaker, especially if you are on the receiving end. This poison will cause the recipient to rapidly fluctuate from the past to the future and back again searching for the why, how, and when of the rumors and hearsay.
  - o Praise, on the other hand, is uplifting. A word of praise delivered with accuracy to the well deserved is one of the greatest Makers.

- **Body language.** A dirty look, an inviting smile, crossed arms of resistance, a disappointed head shake, a warm embrace, and a look of surprise and delight can all affect your S.C.O.R.E. Positive body language can increase S.C.O.R.E., and negative body language can do the opposite.
  - o For example, a friend of mine recently gained employment in a restaurant. After two days of being in the Zone, he noticed his immediate supervisor was scowling with crossed arms. Unaware that her demeanor had nothing to do with him, he became self-conscious and his S.C.O.R.E. plummeted. His performance dropped for the next hour. Her demeanor gnawed on his positive attitude until he asked, "Am I doing all right?" Her reply was "You're doing great. I'm

just having trouble at home." An hour of anguish when the problem wasn't his can do that when negative body language abounds.

o We've all witnessed this next scenario. When time is of the essence, a pivotal teammate falters during a moment of truth. Now a slumped head from the star during the heat of battle quickly permeates his team with lightning-like devastation, and the final result is a loss.

- **Environmental climate** (crowds, people watching you, weather). You'll view many performers at their best and worst when the crowd and television presence is highest, as in the World Series, the Super Bowl, or the Masters. The energy of a crowd can elevate or deflate your mental spirits.

  o Physical surroundings or sudden changes in weather, a flash flood, or a surprise rainfall can all be Breakers. However, viewing a rainbow, a waterfall, or a sunset can be a Maker.

  o Poor lighting in an office can be a Breaker for your overall S.C.O.R.E. Increase the foot-candles of light in the work area, and you'll instantly see the positive difference in the moods of the occupants.

  o Music can change S.C.O.R.E. instantly. While coaching the Honda distributor in the Caribbean, I was observing customers and prospects in one of their showrooms. There was no music for the first three hours I was there. After requesting music, the showroom started to change. You could see people tapping their feet and moving their hands to the rhythm of the beat. During the next three hours, the closing ratio of the sales team doubled. I interviewed all of the customers that were there before and after the music started, and 100 percent said they liked the addition.

- **Luck** (bad bounce, coincidence). This Breaker or Maker seems to come out of nowhere.
    - A bad bounce in tennis can catch us off guard with no warning signals. But a lucky shot where the ball hits the net and then barely trickles over to garner a winning point—that's a Maker!
    - Having a romantic rendezvous only to encounter an old flame at the next table can be a Breaker. "What were the odds?" you think.
    - However, a winning lottery ticket can springboard you to euphoria.

- **Misjudgment** (bad call, misunderstanding, injustice, surprise).
    - Having a boss wrongly misinterpret your last e-mail can be a Breaker.
    - Having an umpire make a bad call when the game is on the line can be a Maker for one team and a Breaker for another.

- **S.C.O.R.E. Level** (partner/teammate/coworker/family/friends).
    - One rotten apple spoils the barrel. And success breeds success. When a loved one is upset and sad, it's nearly impossible not to race to their Low S.C.O.R.E. Level to bail them out. Beware: keep your S.C.O.R.E. balanced.

- **Rhythm change** (delay or interruption).
    - A time-out in a game is designed as a Breaker for the opposition and a Maker for your team. Lightning will scatter golfers from the course, which will stop the momentum of a player on a roll and give a reprieve to the player who can't find the fairway or green. Racing to catch a plane only to encounter a traffic jam can be a Breaker, if we let it.

- **Results** (present tense).
    - o Realizing that you are in first place can be a Breaker for many competitors: "Oh my gosh, I'm beating the club champion." However, it can be a Maker for the champion-to-be, as fear and doubt swiftly evaporate into confidence and poise. Receiving real-time results regarding your business can be a Maker or a Breaker. Realizing you're losing to the worst tennis player in the club can definitely become a Breaker.

        My daughter played junior tennis tournaments growing up. She was winning a match once, only to falter suddenly for no apparent reason. When asked why after her defeat, she replied, "I looked across the net and realized my opponent had a leg brace and an elbow brace. And her glasses looked like they came from the bottom of a Coke bottle. How and why is this match so close?" With that realization, shaking hands at the end of a defeat was the outcome. Typically, when my daughter realized she was playing a close match with an inferior opponent, she used it as a Maker. But not on that day.

- **Arena overlap.** Violating the 90-second rule can contribute to carrying negatives from one arena into another. Thinking about work on the golf course can be a Breaker for your game. Worrying about the whereabouts of your family can definitely take your eye off the ball at work.

Positive or Negative Internal Stimuli

- **Self-expectations** (too high versus too low). "I hope I do well today. I don't want to embarrass myself." These statements before a performance can be a Breaker. Like the brakes on your car, your winning performance can be stopped while returning to your "just do well" expectation. I've coached many competitors who possessed inflated opinions of themselves to the point that their expectations became unrealistic. This was usually coupled with scattered and haphazard preparation. A poor performance usually followed.

- **Individual S.C.O.R.E. components** (too high vs. too low). Any high or low component can act as a solidifying or disruptive force.

- **Experience or results from past performances** (positive vs. negative). "I never play well on the sixteenth hole." "I hate going to your parent's house for dinner." Anchoring your thoughts on a negative past will cause you to project and even magnify these negatives into the future. Worry and anxiety here we come.

- **Knowledge** (client, adversary, product). Not knowing the answer to a product or service question is a death knell for the aspiring sales leader. Knowing the neighborhood shopping, schools, parks, and cultural centers can be a S.C.O.R.E. Maker for the real-estate sales representative.

- **Physical condition** (quantity and quality of sleep, exercise, and nutrition). These Makers and Breakers are obvious on paper but undetectable by most of us until it's too late. Concentration can easily plummet when you're operating on only a few hours sleep. And I've coached many performers who faltered at the end of the performance because of poor nutrition. Athlete or not, we all need the basics of a good night sleep, a balanced diet, and a high standard of physical fitness in order to perform at our best.

- **Future events** (anticipation that causes anxiety, focus, and enthusiasm). How many times have we looked past the performance in front of us and seen the finish line with plenty of race left? "I'm going to win," you'll say. Or "I just have three holes left, and I'll break my personal best." Counting chickens before they're hatched has lost many contests. Also, when you dread the outcome, the present will be greatly affected. A S.C.O.R.E. Maker could occur when you see the finish line as if it's so. It can calm you and give you strength as long as you return to the now before the performance is complete.

- **Love** (romantic or platonic). Yes, this powerful stimulus can be both a Maker and a Breaker. Low self-discipline and concentration can easily be affected with the heart tugs of love. Many times "love run amok" can lower your positive self-esteem as you allow another person to control your thoughts and feelings. Placing all your happy eggs in one basket is very dangerous.

- **Sex.** This opiate can make us travel cross-country to reunite with our beloved, even if for a few minutes. A good friend recently drove six hours one way for a short encounter before returning with a smile just in time for work the next morning. Twelve hours in a car for thirty minutes of. . . . ? A Maker for his Self Arena, maybe, but I'm sure a Breaker for the next day at work. Your conscious mind has only so much room for your daily thoughts. The sex card can trump all other thoughts, regardless of the arena. Channeling your sexual energy into sports, work, or hobbies can have incredible results. Always wanting to act upon these thoughts in a sexual way can definitely be a Breaker in terms of your other arenas.

BREAKER/MAKER CHECKLIST

Retrieve your arena list and mentally peruse each arena for repetitive Makers or Breakers. Go to higher ground. Which person in your Work Arena have you allowed to be a Breaker? What Breakers occur with regularity in your Self Arena? What are the Breakers in your Parent Arena? Are your expectations too high or too low? Acknowledging potential Breakers and repetitive Breakers will assist you in immunizing yourself from negative stimuli while you attract the Zone.

With your external and internal awareness heightened, I know you are ready to run the gauntlet of potential S.C.O.R.E. Breakers. I also believe you are prepared to take advantage of the possible S.C.O.R.E. Makers that abound. With S.C.O.R.E. fortified and fully protected, it's now time to put everything together and unveil the simple S.C.O.R.E. System timeline.

CHAPTER 10

The S.C.O.R.E. System

Would you invest three hours per week to be the best you can be? The average person is awake approximately 112 hours per week (assuming you sleep 8 hours per night). Three hours is less than 3 percent of your waking hours sprinkled over seven days in chunks of a few seconds to a few minutes. I know your answer is yes. So with simplicity and balance as our goals, here's the typical S.C.O.R.E. System timeline.

We are all performers. You perform as a listener and speaker, a buyer or seller, a teacher or student, a participant or spectator. Regardless of the size and importance of a performance, we have time *before, during,* and *after* the performance to prepare, adjust, and evaluate. It's the same time for everyone. Only the true champion uses this time wisely.

First, there is the time before a performance. This is *pre-performance time*. This can be years, months, weeks, days, hours, and minutes before a performance. To prepare our subconscious mind for peak performance, here is a collection of visualization routines I call the Russian Dolls. Once in place, these routines will help you create a Zone overcoat of protection against potential S.C.O.R.E. Breakers. They'll also activate your intuition in guiding your decision making. The Russian Dolls have served all of my clients well in their quest for optimum performance.

<hr>

EXERCISE #38

THE RUSSIAN DOLLS

This collection of time-management routines was created while conducting a seminar in Kiev, Ukraine. It has helped me structure vision, goals, and tasks. It is a specific timeline for preparing and evaluating years, months, weeks, and days. I owe the Russian Dolls for helping me reach the goals in my life.

Years ago, I conducted a seminar for the Ministry of Education for the Ukraine. On my day off, I had the good fortune to purchase souvenirs called nesting dolls. I brought home eight dolls that fit one inside the other, from large to small. The Russian word for nesting doll is matryoshka. *Stemming from the same root as the word* mother, *ma-tryoshka roughly means "little mother." Although nesting dolls have been made in the Far East for many centuries, they were first developed in Russia in the 1890s.*

The dolls became very popular, and soon become a symbol of Mother Russia (maybe you have some). Each doll is carefully turned on a lathe out of a branch of linden wood, then hand-painted, and finally lacquered. Every doll is unique.

I closed my seminar in Kiev by holding the nesting dolls in front of the audience. I began my discussion of my Ukrainian purchase this way.

The largest doll symbolizes your master life vision. *It is special. It is* **large**. *It is unique. It is the mother of all your actions. See this master life vision in your mind frequently, especially before bedtime and just as you awake. This vision should wake you up in the morning and tuck you into bed at night.*

The doll just inside of the largest symbolizes your annual goal. *It is also special. It is still large, but not as large as the vision doll. It fits comfortably inside the first doll. It's unique. See it as it will be. (Every New Year's Eve, find a moment to be alone. With your eyes shut, visualize one year from that moment. See yourself sipping champagne out of a crystal flute glass while celebrating the best year of your life. After opening your eyes, think, "What do I need to accomplish to celebrate like that?" Whatever it is, that is your primary vision for the year.)*

The next doll represents your goal for each quarter of the year *(three months). See your first quarter (January–March) clearly. It is painted by your hands. It is special. It is not as large as the first two dolls, but it is very important. It is unique. (The day before each quarter, find time to be alone. Shut your eyes and visualize the greatest quarter of your life. This vision fits snug inside your annual goal.)*

The fourth doll represents your monthly goals. *It is smaller. It is only 30 days. Thirty days can move swiftly from your calendar. It is seen in your mind a few days before the month begins. It is special. It is unique. See it as it will be. It fits snug inside the quarter doll. (Before every month, visualize the next month as if it's so.)*

The fifth doll symbolizes what you want to accomplish during your week. It's only seven days. One week can pass in the blink of an eye. See this in your mind every Sunday night at the latest. "It's one week from now. What do I want to accomplish?" is your thought. It is special. It is unique. See it as it will be. It fits perfectly inside the monthly doll. (Every Sunday night, find time to be alone and see the next seven days unfold successfully—the greatest week of your life.)

Next is the beautiful doll that reflects one day. *It lasts only 24 hours. Gone. Just like that. Oh, what you can pack inside this doll! See tomorrow's accomplishments during the night before. "I've never lived a day I haven't seen before" is your battle cry. Yes, there will be surprises. Expect them. Prepare for them. This doll is amazing. It is so beautiful. This doll can make a difference in your life and the lives of others. Like a snowflake, there are no two that are alike. It is very special. It is very unique. (Make sure you are alone and relaxed when visualizing the macro items to be accomplished for the next day. This is your Daily Dress Rehearsal.)*

Next is the doll that symbolizes a single performance: *an encounter with friends, family, associates, or prospects; a phone call; a meeting; a round of golf; a tennis match. The average performer may have 40 to 50 performances each week. If you are conducting a meeting, ask, "What do I want these people to think when they drive away alone in their cars?" Whatever you want them to think becomes your agenda for the meeting. When you make an important phone call, think, "What do I want from this phone call once it ends?" Then see it as it will be. Now make the call!*

"When I'm finished with any performance, what have I accomplished?" is your thought. Each performance is unique. They are stand-alones. (If a performance is in a new arena, don't forget the 90-second rule. Visualize results. Conduct a swift S.C.O.R.E. Check.)

Last (but not least) is the smallest doll of all. Through all of the layers of wood and lacquer, it awaits you. The smallest prize. The greatest gift. It's the doll of the moment: *a greeting, a friendly handshake, a putt, a hug, an encounter, a serve in tennis, a good-bye, a moment of silence, an observant eye, an absorbent ear, a spontaneous laugh, a warm smile. "There's no place I'd rather be" is your thought and feeling. In the now.*

This doll is the most special. It is extremely unique. It is magical. Remove this doll, and the others disappear. (The five-second rule will help you stay in the now.)

The Russian dolls. Picture them as your life. You design them to your liking. Each is painted differently. Each belongs inside the other. They fit together. See them as they will be.

Prepare the contents of each of these dolls before the calendar turns to next year. If you haven't started, begin now! Your master life vision doll (the largest one) wakes you up in the morning with a smile and puts you to bed at night with passion for the next day. Spend time with all of the dolls. Just spend more time playing with the small one.

I have encountered many people that have not found their master life vision. My recommendation is to start with a short-term goal of less than six months and then apply the remaining Russian Dolls.

With the visualization routines of the Russian Dolls you will now be better prepared to enter any arena. Remember: *champions win first and then enter the arena.* They are prepared to combat changing conditions and circumstances. They are ready for adversity. *Nonchampions enter the arena and then try to figure out what to do or where to go and how to do it.* They are easily lost and confused when confronted with adversity or moments of truth.

After visualizing each of the Russian Dolls, you only have a few more routines before you enter your next performance.

A salesperson will view the office of a potential client where favorite pictures, awards, plaques, and diplomas are showcased. These items can be addressed during the sales pitch as a S.C.O.R.E. Maker. A tennis player will check out the sun and wind in order to turn them from potential Breakers into Makers. *Remember: S.C.O.R.E. Breakers for some could be Makers for others and vice versa.*

The next routine before a performance is a major S.C.O.R.E. Check. Use this 30- to 90-second routine if time allows before you enter the arena. It's simple. It's like checking the air in your tires before a trip. Too much or too little air in any tire, and the entire ride will be out of balance. Your exercise is to check your S.C.O.R.E. Level before entering your next arena.

EXERCISE #39

PERFORMING A MAJOR S.C.O.R.E. CHECK

- *Self-discipline.* *Divide the performance into manageable bite sizes. When playing golf, break the round into three six-hole sections (beginning, middle, and end). Have goals for each section of the performance. For a meeting, divide it into beginning, middle, and end. Determine how you will start, know the main points to discuss, and close with a call to action from the group. Have strategies and tactics armed and ready. Now you can ask this question: Do I have well-defined goals? The answer is yes or no. If the answer is no, stop right there and correct it. You probably do not need to go further.*

- *Concentration.* *Make up your mind that this is the only place you would rather be. Prepare to be in the now. Know how you will open and close the performance. Now ask these questions: Am I here now? Am I ready to focus my energy? Yes or no?*

- *Optimism.* *Believe in and expect positive results. Also, expect surprises and believe in your ability to handle them—especially adversity. Now ask these questions: Do I believe in me? Do I expect to exit with a positive result? Yes or no?*

- *Relaxation.* *What if I'm nervous? What if I do my S.C.O.R.E. Check and think, "Oh, man, my palms are sweaty. I am so nervous." When you are ready to enter the Zone, all the blood vessels in the stomach constrict, diverting the blood to the brain and the large muscles. (This is the butterflies we mentioned earlier.) Having the butterflies is good; you're getting ready to rock—not choke. If you're feeling uncomfortable with the upcoming performance, don't forget the exercise called Breathe Like a Baby (see page 78). Now ask this question: Am I relaxed? Yes or no?*

- **Enjoyment.** *Prepare to perform with passion and enthusiasm. Now ask these questions: Am I ready to have some fun? Am I excited and enthused?*

After practicing the S.C.O.R.E. Check, you will eventually just ask the simple questions to ascertain your balance or imbalance. With the S.C.O.R.E. Check completed, now, and only now, are you ready to enter the arena. Do this as often as needed. It takes as little as 30 to 90 seconds. It works!

Last, detach yourself from the outcome of the upcoming event or performance. Use the final routine to surrender your performance to your preprogrammed subconscious mind. Trust is the reward from this final action before entering the arena.

<hr style="width:30%">

EXERCISE #40

CLEAR THE LAUNCH

Just before a major performance commences (especially if there is an arena change), do this: Shut your eyes. Unhinge your jaw. Take five or six deep breaths. Turn your mind off and be still (lying down is preferable if possible) for 90 to 120 seconds. See a blank or black screen in your mind. Detach yourself from the outcome of the performance. After nearly two minutes of silence, open your eyes and raise your chin slightly above parallel. The launch is now clear. You are now prepared for a rocket of energy to blast off. You want to clear the launch of all mental clutter and surrender to the almighty subconscious mind. Now open your eyes. *With your eyes engaged in the moment and your chin up in the air, enter the arena as a champion.*

Next up is *performance time.* Let the games begin. This is where the action is. Every performance has an opening, a middle, and a closing. You have already dress-rehearsed for the moment. Open the contest, game, round, meeting, presentation, or conference on your terms. Positive energy! If your energy is flowing with no interruptions, stay the course. When you become aware of a Low S.C.O.R.E. symptom, grab a tool from the S.C.O.R.E. Toolbox (see Appendix A).

Here are a cluster of *universal* tools that you can carry into any performance. When used properly, they can elevate your self-discipline, concentration, optimism, relaxation, and/or enjoyment. Add them to your S.C.O.R.E. Toolbox, where you already have stored individual tools for S.C.O.R.E. *Being able to change a negative to a positive in a matter of seconds sets the S.C.O.R.E. System apart.*

<hr>

EXERCISE #41

CHANGE YOUR BEHAVIOR

This tool may be helpful in raising the level of all of the individual pieces of S.C.O.R.E. if executed in a quick fashion. Like an actor on cue, change your behavior from passive to aggressive or vice versa to keep the sales prospect, student, team, or athletic opponent within your control. For example, slamming on the behavior brakes with a period of silence can be very powerful.

Alter your posture, walking speed, eye focus, hand and face animation, quantity of words, verbal speed, and overall presence. This metamorphosis requires practice and swiftness.

REBOOT THE COMPUTER

This is the same as Clear the Launch, only it is executed in less time. If things are going poorly, not to your liking, use the tool called Reboot the Computer. Shut your eyes. Take a deep breath. Literally turn your mind off. On the screen of space in your mind, see a blank blackboard. Unhinge your jaw. Relax your tongue and be still for 10 to 15 seconds. Then open your eyes, raise your chin above parallel, and start sending energy to your next objective or target. Direct your full focus to the task at hand. This is a reboot; you don't pop the hood of your computer and try to figure it out when it runs slow or freezes. You don't pull out the motherboard and fix it — just reboot it. Some pro golf clients reboot 10 to 15 times during a round. A reboot will last only a few seconds. The longest you would need to reboot would be 30 seconds. That should get your computer, your mind, restarted and refocused.

In addition, the reboot is a great tool to assist you in prolonging the Zone. If things are going well and you become aware of being in the Zone, then reboot. This action will assist you in stretching the time limit of the Zone mind-set.

Say that you are in the middle of a performance, and you've rebooted, changed your behavior from passive to aggressive, and things still aren't clicking. It's time to try the next exercise.

RESTRUCTURE THE SITUATION

Restructuring the situation means that you simply approach the goal in a different way, by changing tactics or strategies. The key is to not violate your style.

I'm very aggressive while playing tennis. I attack. I'm always looking for the opportunity to give my opponent less time. I'm hurrying him or rushing him. If that strategy is not working, I can adjust my attack to a different flank. Attack the forehand as opposed to the backhand. Attack high, low, or down the middle. I can attack slow. I can attack with more pace.

Adjust your style, but never change it.

Loy Vaught of the Los Angeles Clippers called me one night before he was to play center against all-star Hakeem Olajuwon of the world champion Houston Rockets. He was concerned because he would be playing out of position against one of the all-time greats of the game.

That night, Loy armed himself with three tactics, with the second plan to be employed when either Hakeem was in High S.C.O.R.E. or Loy was in Low S.C.O.R.E. His first tactic was to space himself away from the basket in order to draw Olajuwon to the court perimeter. There Loy would shoot his patented 15 to 18 foot jumper from the baseline. "Make him come to me on my terms."

As Hakeem finally adjusted to Loy's court spacing, Loy restructured the situation by driving to the basket. Later, he used his post-up moves to keep this formidable opponent off-balance. Whether the restructuring was tactically sound or not almost didn't matter. The preparation gave Loy the needed confidence to compete at a High S.C.O.R.E. level.

That night, Loy Vaught outscored his personal competition 21 points to 14 and he outrebounded the Houston Hall of Famer by six boards.

Great salespeople are very good at restructuring the situation. Talk about the benefits, not the price. Instead of discussing your service, change tactics and discuss the aftermath of the client receiving your service. Talk about how they will improve their quality of business. Paint that picture in their mind's eye.

Asking a question is the fastest way to restructure, especially if the question is about the person or people you're with. Enter every arena with at least three tactics. One should be your favorite, the one you use

95 percent of the time. Use your second and third tactics to make adjustments when the first one doesn't work. Each tactic should be dress-rehearsed. Timing is the key. Don't wait too long to change gears.

EXERCISE #44

POSITIVE SELF-TALK UNDER FIRE

We've discussed this tool before, in the chapter on optimism (see page 57). Now this positive self-talk — "I sell," "I am accurate," "I hit solid" — can be directed to the obstacle in front of you in the form of a solution. "I" statements are very positive when they are said in the present tense. The statements "I will," "I'm going to," "I shoulda," "I coulda," or "I woulda" are not acceptable. Remember: Your positive "I" statements or affirmations can be silent. They are good tools to use prior to a performance. However, they are great tools when a Breaker appears during the event. For example, say you're in the middle of a sales presentation and the prospect is interrupted by a phone call. He holds up his hand and says, "Hold on just a minute, I'll be right back." This is a possible S.C.O.R.E. Breaker that can change your performance. Use positive, silent self-talk such as "I sell," "I close," "I overcome objections," or "I show benefits" before the meeting starts up again.

EXERCISE #45

THINK S.C.O.R.E.

When the performance is not going your way think the word S.C.O.R.E. to yourself. The thought of the word mentally recreates the feeling of the Zone—that overcoat feeling. As you think of the word S.C.O.R.E., feel the overcoat slip over you and drape you from head to toe with the collar up. Conjure up the feeling of a "purposeful calm."

S.C.O.R.E. SPEED CHECK

You know this tool. It is the shortened version. Use it only if time permits while the performance is in progress. Once you find the weak link, stop there. Awareness will mend your S.C.O.R.E. Level the majority of the time. This will take 30 seconds or less.

Ask yourself the following questions. Do I have . . .

S: Goals? Well-defined targets? Commitment? Patience?

C: Directed energy? Cheetah focus? Tunnel vision?

O: Belief? Expectancy? Trust?

R: Controlled breathing? Unhinged jaw? Comfort? Peace?

E: Movement? Enthusiasm? Passion?

SEE THE FINISH

This tool takes a maximum of five seconds. When the performance is not to your liking, quickly see the positive conclusion in your mind in a finished state—as if it's so. Then swiftly get back to the task at hand. In the now.

In the middle of a performance when the momentum has shifted to your opponent, try this exercise. A tennis player sees the opponent netting a forehand on match point. Trailing at halftime, a coach briefly sees the final score with his team jumping with joy. With the outcome of the presentation in doubt, the salesperson sees a signed contract with a check. A golfer may see the victory celebration. Remember, after a quick five-second mental view of the finish, return to the trench of the battle and remain detached from the outcome until the conclusion.

Martha Nause had a vision. She had played on the LPGA Tour for 17 years and never came close to winning a major golf tournament. In fact, her main goal each week was just to survive the cut. She lived week to week with this mind-set until we met in 1994. Martha spent six days practicing the S.C.O.R.E. System. Her vision was to win an LPGA event. She immersed herself in improving her daily routines, and soon she was talking, walking, and playing like a champion. Every day she practiced seeing herself holding the winner's check. You know . . . the whopping monster check that takes two people to hold at the award ceremony.

On the sixth day, I said, "You're ready to win." Her talent was not in question. It was her mind-set that was her major stumbling block. I told her, "I believe and expect you to win the next event." She replied, "But it's the du Maurier, the fourth LPGA major tournament." I had never heard of the event. Without emotion, I said, "Now play the game inside the game. You're prepared. Use S.C.O.R.E. to keep you in the present tense." With the formula etched in her mind like indelible ink, she boarded a flight to Canada.

The first night of the tournament, she called me, extremely excited. "I set the course record!" she screamed into the phone. "I'm leading the tournament!" "Great job," I replied. "But that's not your vision or goal. Get back inside the game. Stay on course. Use the tools to keep you in the present tense. Good night." I hung up on her.

On Sunday Martha was three shots off the lead with four holes to go. She was playing with the leaders with the world watching. As the moment of truth stared her in the eye, she started to panic. Then she called on her vision. She shut her eyes on the fifteenth tee and an image appeared. She saw herself holding up the winner's check. The last three holes were surreal. Everything appeared to be in slow motion. She felt a "purposeful calm" come over her. Before she knew it the $120,000 prize was hers. And there she stood with the oversized check high above her head. In Martha's long career the most prize money she had won for a season was $76,000. And in one glorious weekend she almost doubled it. She was a champion with a champion's vision. Sometimes you just need to see the finish.

Colony Marine is a powerboat dealer outside of Detroit, Michigan. When a performance or a day does not reach their standards, the key management team individually thinks 60–5–3. These simple numbers represent their financial goals for the year. 60–5–3 is the financial combination to unlock an impressive annual performance. Briefly seeing the finish gets them back on track toward their goals.

EXERCISE #48

MENTOR IMAGE

See your mentor (mother, father, big brother or sister, coach, teacher, or positive role model) in your mind. Hear his favorite words of encouragement. See his positive body language. He symbolizes peak performance. He will always motivate you and keep you going strong. I still visualize Professor Ross saying, "Close like a champion. Close!"

Again, add these universal tools to the individual tools you've learned for each component of S.C.O.R.E.

Last is *post-performance time*—where the evaluation takes place. Most performers evaluate poorly or not at all when they are victorious. And when they lose, many scrutinize and belabor every missed opportunity and poor decision to the point of overanalysis. Treat winning and losing the same in terms of evaluation. By employing consistent evaluations for your performances, days, weeks, and months, learning will be maximized. Champions enter the past for learning *only*.

<hr>

EXERCISE #49

PERFORMANCE EVALUATIONS
(BE OBJECTIVE)

There are three types of performance evaluations: (1) Quick, (2) Standard; and (3) In-depth. Listen to your intuition as you evaluate. Let it override all thoughts of logic as you review your performance. Listen to your gut!

1. *This* Quick Evaluation *is for phone calls, e-mails, short one-on-one meetings, and brief group encounters. It takes less than 30 seconds. Here time is of the essence. Immediately upon completing the short performance, ask yourself:*
   a. *Did I accomplish my objective?*
   b. *What would I do differently?*
   c. *What action will occur from the performance? Mentally, see this dynamic happening as if it's so.*
   d. *How was my S.C.O.R.E.?*

2. *The* Standard Evaluation *is for longer performances. It needs approximately two to five minutes. Ask yourself the following questions immediately after the performance:*

a. *What do the participants (opponents) think now?*

b. *What actions will take place?*

c. *Did I accomplish my goals? If not why?*

d. *What is my S.C.O.R.E. Level? Rate it from 1 to 10 (10 is high).*

e. *What was my weakest link in S.C.O.R.E.?*

f. *What is the S.C.O.R.E. Level of the participants or opponents? Rate it from 1–10 (10 is high).*

g. *What S.C.O.R.E. Breakers or Makers occurred?*

h. *What tools were used or needed to be used?*

i. *What do I need to do to prepare for my next performance?*

3. *Here is a sample* In-depth Evaluation *sheet. Take your time answering each question.*

Performance: _____

Date: _____

Time: _____

Place: _____

Situation: _____

Evaluate your performance by asking the following:

1. *Did I prepare well? Yes or no. If not, what do I need to do differently?*

2. *Were my visualizations accurate?*

3. *Rate my S.C.O.R.E. Level on a 1–10 scale before the event (10 is high).*

4. *Rate my S.C.O.R.E. Level on a 1–10 scale during the event (10 is high).*

5. *Were my routines satisfactory?*

6. *Did I open the performance(s) in the present tense?*

7. *Did I establish my rhythm and tempo?*

8. *Did I establish my strategy at the beginning?*
9. *What S.C.O.R.E. Breakers (if any) occurred before the event?*
10. *What S.C.O.R.E. Breakers (if any) occurred during the event?*
11. *What S.C.O.R.E. Makers (if any) occurred before the event?*
12. *What S.C.O.R.E. Makers (if any) occurred during the event?*
13. *What Tool Box techniques did I use? Did they work?*
14. *Did I reach High S.C.O.R.E. and/or the Zone?*
15. *Which fundamental performance techniques do I need to practice? (This depends on the arena and may not be applicable to the S.C.O.R.E. System, though it does influence the System.)*
16. *Were my problems mental, physical, or technical?*
17. *What did I learn for use in future performances?*
18. *What were my opponent's strengths? (May not apply.)*
19. *What successful strategies did they employ? (May not apply.)*
20. *Did I reach my personal performance standard? If not, which S.C.O.R.E. elements were below par?*

Finally, evaluate your S.C.O.R.E. Level after every performance, day, week, month, quarter, and year.

The question "How was my S.C.O.R.E.?" is simple. Was it more toward the High or Low? What was the weak link? Is there a pattern? Learn from your performance. Extract the golden nuggets of knowledge from your efforts. See this newfound information incorporated into your next performance. Bury the nonimportant residue in your mental graveyard, then move on with wisdom tucked under your arm as you prepare for your next performance, day, week, month, quarter, or year.

Remember: all of your performances are spread over multiple life arenas. A true champion reviews his arenas by going to

> **Losses are lessons learned by the champion.**

higher ground at least once each week. After taking your mental inventory of positive and negative and future and past tense or the week, you will be better prepared for your next per-

w have routines for preparing a year, a quarter, a month, a
, u day, or a performance. Repetition will ensure that your
S.C.O.R.E. will stay balanced most of the time. You are armed with a
collection of tools that can adjust any performance. You have multiple
checklists for evaluating like a champion. You are on a fast track of
learning that will carry you victorious to the finish line. You are now
thinking like a true champion.

THE S.C.O.R.E. SYSTEM

Daily

- See your master life vision (as you wake).
- S.C.O.R.E. Check (a.m.).
- Pre-performance routines.
  1. Visualize results
  2. Screen for Breakers/Makers
  3. S.C.O.R.E. Check
  4. Clear the Launch
- Performance routines.
  1. Open on your terms
  2. Use the Tool Box for adjustments
  3. Close like a champion
- Post-performance routines.
  1. Evaluate
  2. Retool for next performance
- Daily Dress Rehearsal (next day)
- S.C.O.R.E. Check (p.m.)
- See your master life vision (as you drift into sleep).

Weekly

- Go to higher ground (Arena Review)
- S.C.O.R.E. evaluation (for past 7 days)
- Weekly Russian Doll

Monthly

- S.C.O.R.E. evaluation (last 30 days)
- Monthly Russian Doll

Quarterly

- S.C.O.R.E. evaluation (last 30 days)
- Quarterly Russian Doll

Are you ready to manage your S.C.O.R.E. Level? Are you ready to S.C.O.R.E. for life?

CHAPTER 11

"WYOU, You're on the Air"

Within 10 days of using the S.C.O.R.E. System, you will become aware of coincidence, good luck, synchronicity, and uncanny occurrences in your life. You will realize that your brain works like a television transmitter and receiver. That's right! Every thought you have is being broadcasted with your physical, emotional, and intuitive cues.

Every day, you mentally house thousands of thoughts. These thoughts are kinetic energy that produces subtle vibrations in the brain. These vibrations can and will be received by everyone around you, as well as people miles away. These vibes are deciphered into visual images from the intuitive portion of the brain.

Has this ever happened to you? You start thinking of an old friend (seeing him in your mind), and within the same day he calls you out of the blue. Your response is "I was just thinking about you." Coincidence? Maybe . . . but probably not! Your brain works like a television broadcasting system. The more an idea, person, or concept repeats in your mind, backed by belief and expectancy, the more your subconscious will attempt to manifest it.

How real is your vision in your mind? Can you see it? Are you repetitious? Believe it. Expect it. And then put on your seat belt. When I was 14 years old, I was sitting on a park bench overlooking the tennis courts in Ashland, Kentucky, reading an article in a tennis magazine. It was a diary written by two young Italian tennis players about their international travels. They were my age. While I was reading the article, Professor Ross walked behind me and stopped to peer over my shoulder. He said nothing. The next day at about the same time, I was reading the very same article and the professor again walked behind me and peered over my shoulder. He then said, "Go there. Play tennis with these boys in your mind. Travel with them. Play with them. See it as it will be." I replied that I didn't understand. He repeated, "Play tennis with those boys in your mind. See the movie. Make the movie what you want."

That night I went home and thought about playing tennis with those Italian boys. I didn't think about them every night that summer, but I did think about them a lot. "See it as it will be" were the professor's words of encouragement. Twelve years later, with Appalachia far behind, I coached those boys (Adriano Panatta and Paolo Bertolucci) on the Italian Davis Cup team that lost in the world Davis Cup finals to the United States. We traveled the world together. Coincidence? Not hardly. Synchronicity? Absolutely. "All great men can see the future in their minds," said the professor. He was right. Visualization became my newest tool, and I've been honing it for a lifetime.

Your mental computer storehouse is relentless. It will hunt for every way to make your dreams come true. However, repetitious thoughts of poverty will cause your mind to pursue poverty, despair, or disappointment. The subconscious is a problem-solving machine. But remember, it doesn't care if your thoughts are good or bad. It will cause manifestation into its physical equivalent. Whatever images occur repeatedly on its screen of space.

Has this ever happened? You are at lunch with a friend, and you can't think of the name of a song. You can hear the tune in your mind, but the title escapes you. You say, "It's a Beatles' song. It's on the tip of my tongue." After a few random guesses from your friend, you change the subject and eventually finish dinner with the nameless song long forgotten. Several hours later with other friends at dinner, you blurt out, "A Hard Day's Night." This is said out loud with blank, dumbfounded looks appearing on the face of everyone at the table. "Oh, that's just a song I was trying to think of all day," you reply. What a machine! Multitasking throughout the day, unnoticed, until it solved your problem and delivered the goods without fail. Once your subconscious believes and expects your thought, it will comb your mental file cabinet or the file cabinet of others until it reaches its goal. The good news is all of your thoughts are being broadcast. Of course, the bad news is all of your thoughts are being broadcast.

The following has been my favorite observation over the past three decades. With the arrival of the new millennium, I believe I will witness this occurrence with greater regularity.

We have a field of energy that surrounds us 360 degrees. This field expands and contracts according to our thoughts. All thought is kinetic energy. Think positive, and it expands. Think negative, and it contracts.

Many people can expand their energy by as much as several hundred feet ahead of them. It serves as their pathway. Sometimes this field can enter the room before they physically do. Every person in this imaginary path of energy can feel it. They may not know where it came from, but they can tell there is a difference in the air. I've witnessed this occurrence many times.

I observed this phenomenon when Michael Jordan was chasing his baseball dream. I was in the Chicago White Sox locker room in their spring training camp in Sarasota, Florida. The room was filled with baseball players. A few were engaged in small talk. Some were at their respective lockers. People were walking in and out. Suddenly, I looked up from my thoughts as if I had been tapped on the shoulder. The room looked the same, but I noticed electricity in the air that hadn't been there before. The chatter had increased. People smiled. There was an enthusiasm spiraled that hadn't been there before. Physically, nothing in the room had changed.

Within seconds, Michael walked into the room. Silence. Then he started talking. The room filled with an energy that is still difficult to explain.

What happened? How can some people command attention before and after they enter a room? They don't have to speak a word. Their presence sends an energy charge through everyone in attendance.

In the late seventies, I recorded many moments when this invisible field of energy filled a room before the sender walked through the door. For seven years, while coaching full-time on the ATP men's tennis tour, I observed Arthur Ashe, Bjorn Borg, Ivan Lendl, and Jimmy Connors exhibiting this energy projection. Their energy flow was especially prevalent when they were on top of their games. Jack Nicklaus had this ability. I saw him project this energy at the Masters as I sat on the clubhouse veranda, watching him enter the porch area. Tiger Woods has extended his field of energy to tremendous proportions. I felt it in the locker room, practice green, and fairways in many PGA tournaments in 2000. His competitors felt it as they collectively wilted in his presence.

Sports superstars used this power long before they achieved celebrity status. It's one of the main reasons they reached the pinnacle of success.

Energy projection is not limited to great athletes. All of us possess the power to expand our own energy fields. In fact, at every wedding

I've attended, the bride possessed the ability to mesmerize the crowd as she walked down the aisle. We can witness this phenomenon at birthday parties, award dinners, concerts, and other events. There are several secrets to this phenomenon.

First, the people with this penetrating aura possess only positive thoughts. They are filled to the maximum with confidence and optimism. You very rarely hear negative words or expressions from these performers. Their S.C.O.R.E. Level is balanced.

Second, they project this positive energy outward. They feel magnetized. Because of their life preparations, they spend more time in the present tense. It is present-tense energy that can be felt by most in the awaiting arena or room.

Next, they expect positive results from everyone around them. They especially expect high standards from their teammates. And because they see the positives in every teammate, their teammates respond. Magic Johnson (Los Angeles Lakers) and Larry Bird (Boston Celtics) were both world champions that possessed this ability. Jack Welch of General Electric also possessed this ability to elevate his team into the Zone. And so did Mother Teresa as she toiled in poverty, lifting the spirits of the downtrodden in Calcutta, India.

Last, these energized performers expect positive outcomes for themselves regardless of the situation.

Everyone possesses the ability to broadcast this energy field. The results from repetitive use of this power will amaze you. Here are some guidelines based on my observations.

EXERCISE #50

ENERGY FIELD GUIDELINES

1. *Carry yourself in an erect posture with your head placed high over your sternum. Walk with an assured gait, like you're going somewhere specific.*

2. *Speak less. Listen and observe more.*

3. *Fill your thoughts with positives. Eliminate worry, doubt, and assumption thinking. Avoid negative body language, sarcasm, gossip, and ridicule.*

4. *Practice the Golden Rule: Do unto others as you would have them do unto you.*

5. *When you offer an introductory handshake, look the other person in the eye while clasping her hand. Hold the handshake long enough to ascertain her eye color (but remember, if you look at her too long she might feel uncomfortable). State your name slowly and clearly while the handshake is still firm. Pause between your first name and last name: for example, "My name is James [pause] Bond." Attentiveness increases 40 percent with this simple pause between your first and last name. Repeat the other person's name out loud after she introduces herself. Every recipient of your handshake should feel your vibrant, positive energy. And everyone needs to remember your name.*

6. *When you enter a room, scour the surroundings. Make eye contact. Observe with all of your senses.*
7. *Replace all intuitively received negative thoughts with a warm, sincere smile.*
8. *Turn the expressionless or negative-looking body language of the people you meet into smiling faces and positive body language.*
9. *Using visualization, change negative people into positive life forces. If they have a history of being moody and sullen, change them with your positive manner and thoughts. See them as happy and enthusiastic.*
10. *Use positive animated gestures. Smile! Force everyone to smile.*
11. *Use silence more than words.*
12. *Keep your S.C.O.R.E. balanced.*

Like a champion, increase your field of energy.

You broadcast your S.C.O.R.E. Level every minute of your life. If you have a Low S.C.O.R.E. Level or you're stuck in the Downs, your transmission can frighten away the girl you're trying to ask out on a date. If your S.C.O.R.E. Level is high, it may stimulate a potential car buyer into making one of the biggest purchases of his life.

Whatever your broadcast, those around you sense your positive or negative vibes. Positives repel negatives. Negatives repel positives.

With planning, you can transmit any thought to the target of your choice. How can you be sure he'll receive your transmission? Trust is the only answer. Trust based on belief and expectancy.

Everyone receives subconscious vibrations from other people, but only a few act on it. Remember, you have 2,000 to 3,000 thoughts each day, 60 percent of them chaotic. But half of your chaotic thoughts didn't originate in your mind. That's right. Approximately 600 to 900 thoughts a day are flowing from people you know and don't know. For example: A stranger owns a patent for an injection molding machine. He sees it being distributed globally. He believes and expects this to happen. You own a distribution and sales organization with many international factories as clients.

One day in Chicago, you bump into each other in an elevator. You strike up a conversation and end up solidifying a joint venture over time. Coincidence? Absolutely not! This is happening every day with millions of people. You have intuitive thoughts on a daily basis. From time to time, you've probably said, "I have good vibes about him" or "I have bad vibes about my trip." Most nonchampions dismiss it as coincidence or luck. Many are guided to the opportunity, but most don't see it.

Do you act on your intuition?

Many baseball pitchers shake off the signs given to them by their catcher during a crucial part of the game. They have a gut feeling that they need to throw a different pitch. Sometimes they accept his sign and throw the pitch without their own personal conviction. When they don't listen to their intuition, they make mistake after mistake.

In 1998, I coached six major-league pitchers. They collectively reported to me 86 instances when they failed to listen to their intuition. This failure to act on their gut feeling or intuitive vibe cost them 92 percent of the time. Of those failures, their opponents took advantage of them with base hits, stolen bases or walks, and resulted in my client's removal from the game.

Your mind is in possession of a spectacular transmitter and receiver. It's your television station. You are the owner, station manager, program director, and announcer. You decide the format, content, and program duration.

Champions control their stations with the highest frequency of positive vibes. They broadcast their innermost thoughts in finished, solution-oriented states. They see themselves as winners, and they send everyone this image. Their positive transmissions also allow them to receive answers to their problems. These answers will arrive while they're preparing for and during their performance. And then they act on their intuitions.

What can you communicate through these broadcasts?

You can broadcast anything and everything, regardless of whether it's good or bad. You can broadcast to anyone who's in the now, especially if that person listens to her intuition. If the recipient is worried about the past or anxious regarding the future, the transmission can get garbled or lost. Also, she will likely not realize the communication is from you.

When your thoughts are your own and are backed by belief, expectancy, and repetition, your transmissions will continuously broadcast until received and acted upon.

You will receive answers, solutions, or physical manifestations to your transmissions as hunches or intuitive thoughts minutes, hours, days, or weeks after a broadcast transmission. Your transmission goes into a universal pool of intelligence. When the right answer arises, it will hit you with a sheer force as if it lay right at your feet the entire time.

It's like Professor Ross used to tell me: "When you're ready to learn, answers will appear." Listen to your gut!

When is the best time to send and receive these vibrations?

Transmit your thoughts just before you go to sleep, just as you awake, and/or in any induced state of relaxation. It's imperative to broadcast during these drowsy states of mind, otherwise known as *alpha* states. These are the most conducive times for harmonious mind-body connectivity. When your subconscious being is most ready for change, it accepts more ideas as its own. Dozens of my clients actively energize their teammates and de-energize the opposition with their transmission of positive energy.

The opposition will have a feeling that they must play better than normal. They feel like they need to try harder. Where does this feeling originate? It emanates from the conscious and subconscious mind of your broadcasts.

Most champions have the uncanny ability to read the arena situation and make timely adjustments at the right time and place.

"I knew what he was going to throw."
"I had a sense they would low ball the deal."

This is also the reason why some people you know always seem to run into bad luck. It's the reason for sustained poverty, loneliness, and unhappiness.

"I can't win for losing."
"Life's unfair."

These negative broadcasts verbally, nonverbally, and intuitively emanate from a Low S.C.O.R.E. Level or the Downs. They repel the opportunity for success and attract the negative forces that shackle your abilities.

Now, make this form of positive visualization a part of the S.C.O.R.E. process. Remember that you possess free will. Program a positive broadcast. Increase your field of energy. It's your station: "WYOU, you're on the air."

CHAPTER 12

Fannin's Final Word

The S.C.O.R.E. Performance System philosophy is to *"invest in the future so you can reap the rewards now."* Visualize. See the future in your mind as it will be. Then walk an illuminated pathway to success with awareness in case an adjustment is necessary.

The S.C.O.R.E. System is a collection of thought-management tools designed to reach any goal or vision. Because you have free will, you have the power to change yourself. From negative to positive . . . the choice is yours.

By changing yourself first, you will have the ability to influence the thoughts of others. This is power!

We are all born differently. Some of us have different skin and eye color, physiques, intelligence, appetites, personality, race, heritage, and religious upbringing. Just like the different models of cars on the road, we are different on our particular road of life. Some of us are Ferraris—sleek, fast, quick, and stylish. Those fortunate enough to be born a Ferrari have a great personality, a high IQ, perfect teeth (no dentist necessary), and natural six-pack abs. Others are born as clunkers—they're just like the simple, no-frills automobiles you see on the highway. These people have crooked teeth, a low IQ, and a dull personality, and are adorned with a keg instead of six-pack abs.

Most of us are somewhere in between these models. Just as we are different in size, shape, and performance capability, we also have different paths or roads. These paths, unlike our bodies, can be chosen. While traveling our road, some of us unwittingly choose as our destination the states of despair, poverty, hardship, divorce, bankruptcy, and abuse. Others choose the states of happiness, wealth, love, health, and overall well-being. All of this is because in everyone's car there are *three* potential drivers. And only *one* can drive at any given time. You know all three drivers.

First, there is the *judge*. When the judge drives, he's too busy to watch the road. That's because he's watching the other cars and drivers, judging their performance and how they look. The judge doesn't take advantage of the straightaways in life because he doesn't keep his eye on the road. This driver is very inefficient and slow.

You know the second driver in your car. It's the *victim*. When the victim drives, he's always complaining about the car, the road conditions, the congested traffic, and everything else that circumstance and conditions cause. When the victim drives your car, you never get to your destination on time, if at all.

And by now, you fully know the third driver in the car—the *true champion*. When the true champion drives, the first thing she does is pull a road map from the glove compartment and find point A and point B. She sees a straight path and begins the journey with belief and expectancy. She has self-discipline with a clear vision of her destination. She has faith in her ability to get there. On the straightaways, she floors the accelerator and races at top speed, keeping her eye on the road. She concentrates well. With a sense of being in the moment, she slows down and hugs the curves for efficiency and safety, while the victim and the judge are complaining about the terrain. They wonder if they are on the wrong pathway. If an object falls in the middle of the road, the true champion runs over it if it's small, goes around it if it's too big, or gets out of the car and removes it if it's too cumbersome. The true champion exudes optimism, while the victim is upset with the delay and the judge complains about who would leave this obstacle in the road. Both are pessimistic about reaching their destination. They expect problems. And if the true champion is tired, she pulls off the road and rests, while the victim complains about someone keeping him awake all night, and the judge worries that there is no place to pull over.

The true champion enjoys the journey. If the driver of another car is being reckless and is rude with obscene gestures, the victim's day is ruined, while the judge screams, "You idiot!" at the top of his lungs. The true champion dismisses the reckless driver. She does not allow the beautiful scenery to be missed and her S.C.O.R.E. Level to plummet. Finally, the victim and the judge complain, gossip, and moan about everyone on the road, as well as every wrong turn and dead end. The true champion drives off in the Zone.

You need to decide each and every day who's driving your car. Is it the *victim?* Is it the *judge?* Or is it the *true champion?*

Many centuries ago, a peaceful tribe from a small island nation (suffered an annual attack) after their yearly harvest by a combative tribe from another island. Each fall, their land was pillaged. The emotional and physical pain inflicted was great, and it left scars that were visible in the eyes of the vanquished.

After many sad and defenseless years of succumbing to their attackers, the chieftain of the peaceful tribe spoke: "Enough! We will not run, hide, or fight on our land again." He called for a surprise attack on the soil of the transgressors.

His men were mollified.

The next day at dawn, they set sail leaving their wives and children behind. After a treacherous sea voyage, they reached the shores of their nemesis. Shortly thereafter, the tribal head made another alarming request.

"Burn the boats!" bellowed the defiant leader. "What?" his men replied in disbelief. With stoic demeanor, the chieftain repeated, "Burn the boats so we can't retreat to the sea. Live or be killed. There will be no turning back. Burn the boats! We'll defeat them and return with their boats and spoils."

The overmatched nation of farmers and seamen overcame their once superior foes through surprise, daring, and tenacity, and by eliminating all options except success.

Now I want *you* to "burn the boats" to your past. Burn the boats to negative thinking. Burn the boats to being "normal." Burn the boats to the victim and the judge. And burn the boats while moving on with your life with conviction, determination, and passion.

Montgomery Ward didn't burn the boats. It remained the same until the bitter end. Oldsmobile didn't burn the boats, and its cars are no longer on the road. Eastern Airlines didn't burn the boats, and its planes were sold to the highest bidder. Hundreds of other companies didn't burn their boats, either. And neither are many other corporate icons that will be going down soon because of archaic thinking.

It's time to reinvent yourself. Use your imagination. Apply the Golden Rule. Think only positive thoughts. Stop procrastinating. Invest in the future so that you can reap the rewards today.

Abnormal goals require abnormal thinking.

Do a kind deed. Get disciplined. Walk the walk and talk the talk. Go for it. It's time to be heard. It's time to make a difference. It's time to be persistent. Focus like the cheetah. It's time to share. Eliminate gossip, rumor, and hearsay from your life. Live with passion. Quit complaining. Treat yourself like a champion. Tell the truth. It's time to act. Remove the bumper sticker that reads "Think Global . . . Act Local" and just do it. It's time to relax during "moment of truth" situations. Live in the present tense. Look people in the eye and tell them what you want. It's time to have faith. Say, "I'm sorry," to an old friend. Boycott gossip magazines and television shows. It's time to say, "This is not acceptable!" to the monopolies of the world. It's time to be wealthy. Write your novel. Buy your dream house. Take your company to the next level. Run the marathon. Fix your teeth. Lose weight. Bury the hatchet with an old friend or a relative. Ask your boss for a raise. Change careers. Take a world cruise. Head for Broadway. Leave a bad relationship. Keep a journal. Say no to whatever you've reluctantly said yes to before. Say yes to whatever you've reluctantly said no to before.

It's time to mend fences and heal old wounds. It's time to be the best friend you can be. It's time to focus. It's time to teach old dogs new tricks. It's time to be healthy. Be patient. Nurture your spiritual being. Be physically fit. Be a good neighbor. It's time to lead. Treat the elderly with reverence. Think like a true champion. Make peace with your maker. It's time to look in the mirror at your best friend. It's time you balance your S.C.O.R.E.

It's time.

Chin up. Eyes forward. Jaw unhinged. No looking back.

Good fortune favors the bold. It's time to use the S.C.O.R.E. System to improve your life and the lives of others. It's time to get in the Zone. It's time to S.C.O.R.E. for Life.

DON'T FORGET TO TAKE THE S.C.O.R.E. FOR LIFE FINAL EXAM TO SEE HOW YOU STACK UP AGAINST THE TRUE CHAMPION'S MIND.

S.C.O.R.E. FOR LIFE FINAL EXAM

This is a quiz to see how your thoughts stack up against the true champion. Answer them honestly. Rate the following statements on a scale of 1 to 5 (5 is high). Add the total of the statements to determine which S.C.O.R.E. component is out of balance.

5- Always True, 4- Often True, 3- Sometimes True,
2- Seldom True, 1- Never or Almost Never True

Self-Discipline

_____ 1. I am prepared before my performances.

_____ 2. I evaluate objectively after my performances.

_____ 3. I make positive adjustments during my performances.

_____ 4. I have well-defined performance goals that are measurable.

_____ 5. I am patient with my pre-performance, performance, and post-performance time.

TOTAL: _____

Concentration

_____ 1. I focus well during my pre-performance time.

_____ 2. I am not easily distracted during a performance.

_____ 3. I see my goals with clarity.

_____ 4. I perform in the present tense.

_____ 5. I focus all of my energies toward my customers, associates, or opponents.

TOTAL: _____

Optimism

_____ 1. I believe in me.

_____ 2. I expect to perform at least at my daily standard.

_____ 3. I make positive adjustments to performance conditions and situations.

_____ 4. *I win in my mind before I compete.*

_____ 5. *My verbal and nonverbal communications are positive.*

TOTAL: _____

Relaxation

_____ 1. *I am comfortable with adverse conditions.*

_____ 2. *I perform with ease and relative calm.*

_____ 3. *I make my associates comfortable and relaxed when I'm around them.*

_____ 4. *I perform without worry or anxiety.*

_____ 5. *I perform at my own rhythm and tempo.*

TOTAL :_____

Enjoyment

_____ 1. *I show high enthusiasm before, during, and after my performances.*

_____ 2. *I love to perform in competitive situations.*

_____ 3. *I have passion while preparing for my performances.*

_____ 4. *I enjoy solving performance problems.*

_____ 5. *I reflect enjoyment in my verbal and nonverbal communications.*

TOTAL: _____

S_____ C_____ O_____ R_____ E_____ =
TOTAL S.C.O.R.E._____

The lowest numerical score for the individual S.C.O.R.E. component is your current weakest link. Now check how your total score stacks up against the true champion's mind.

FINAL EXAM RESULTS

119–125: *You are mentally a world-class performer. You have great preparation, performance adjustments, and objective evaluations. You know who you are, where you want to* *go, and how to get there. Stay on course. Stay balanced, and keep it simple.*

113–118: *Excellent! You are a Zone performer. Keep it up! Don't forget to take periodic rest, relaxation, and retooling breaks. Your necessary areas of growth are few. Small adjustments in thinking will take you to the top. Believe in and expect the best of yourself.*

100–112: *You are a solid performer. You are on your way. You seldom perform below your daily standard. However, you will need a better effort if you are to compete with the best when it counts the most. Visualize winning. Deal from strength mentally, physically, or technically. Good fortune favors the bold.*

88–99: *You are an average performer. You need to improve one or all of your S.C.O.R.E. components if you want to compete with the best. Sharpen your goals. Make them measurable and crystal clear. Repetition of positive routines will get you going. Be patient but persistent. Relax when you need to. You may be trying too hard.*

75–87: *You are performing below normal standards. Your performances need immediate attention and repair. You are probably performing on a roller coaster of highs and lows. Prepare more thoroughly! Check for expectations set too high or too low.*

63–74: *You are cannon fodder for the confident foe. Potential customers will sense your low S.C.O.R.E. Level and gravitate elsewhere. You need to reevaluate your vision and corresponding goals. Soul-search your level of belief and expectancy. You must change any negative thinking. You definitely need to improve the quality of pre-performance, per-*

formance, and post-performance time. You may need to consider alternative quests. Seek quality assistance through continued education, financial backing, new resources, and support from family and friends.

62 and under: *You are not in the game. If this score persists, either change the goal or approach it in a completely different way. You are on the wrong path.*

The Toolbox

Many people want a quick Zone fix. Here is an easy-to-reference list of the tools, exercises and quizzes in the book.

S.C.O.R.E. Review

Know the definition of each S.C.O.R.E. component. They are as follows:

Self-discipline: the willingness and commitment to stay with a task(s) to reach well-defined goals that lead to a vision. A person with high self-discipline possesses vision, well-defined goals, control, patience, persistence, strategy, tactics, and positive time management.

Concentration: the ability to focus mental and physical energy on the task(s) to reach well-defined goals that lead to a vision. A person with high concentration possesses focus, tunnel vision, efficiency, accuracy, productivity, and quality.

Optimism: the belief and expectancy that one can execute the task(s) to reach well-defined goals that lead to a vision. A person with high optimism possesses confidence, positive self-esteem, trust, knowledge, faith, and expectancy.

Relaxation: being mentally and physically comfortable (free from worry or anxiety) with the task(s) to reach well-defined goals that lead to a vision. A person with high relaxation possesses calm, ease, peace, tranquility, comfort, smoothness, and grace.

Enjoyment: the satisfaction and/or pleasure of executing the task(s) to reach well-defined goals that lead to a vision. A person with high enjoyment possesses fun, happiness, joy, enthusiasm, passion, excitement, high energy, zest, and pleasure.

S.C.O.R.E. for . . .
(and Other Closing Thoughts)

Sales

A company sales manager was having problems with his sales force. There were many nonproducers that were starting to frustrate him. He had been the number one salesman in the company for years before he was promoted. He knew what it took to be successful. He knew about performing in the Zone, and was disappointed his sales force couldn't or wouldn't follow his lead. However, the former sales star couldn't place himself in each of his fellow coworker's shoes.

Everyone had different reasons for working for the company. Everyone had one or more missing ingredients of S.C.O.R.E. that kept him or her from reaching high daily standards.

After I coached this sales captain for 10 days, he abandoned his traditional group sales meetings and embarked on one-on-one coaching himself. He mentally fired everyone in his division and rehired them while he changed his attitude. He listened and observed. His meetings focused on the customer, not his staff. Every individual meeting was centered on how the individual salesman could bond with the customer. He assisted each salesperson in thinking about what they needed to think about.

He never mentioned his old days of selling again. After 30 days, he returned to his traditional group meetings. Within three months, his division broke all company records, and three of his staff shattered his old sales marks. By improving his team's S.C.O.R.E. Levels, he orchestrated a balance that attracted the Zone.

Coaching

Several years ago, I was in a private session with Doc Rivers, then the coach of the Orlando Magic. I asked him who his favorite coach was when he was a player in the NBA and what was his most memorable moment. Without hesitation, he told me the following story.

"I was playing for Coach Pat Riley as a member of the New York Knicks. We were locked in a play-off battle with Michael Jordan and the Chicago Bulls. We found ourselves down by 22 points at the half as we walked into our locker room with dejection and disgust. Coach Riley gathered us in the corner of the room as close as we could get. He pulled a chair in front and sat down looking at each of us with a sweeping glare.

"Many on our team started small talk about our first-half play, with a few even making wisecracks about how close Riley had gathered us. Coach remained stoic and silent.

"After six or seven minutes of silence from Pat Riley, our team fell silent as well. No one said a word. We immediately realized that no instructions were going to be given . . . no thoughts from the first half were going to be expressed. With silence, Coach made it clear that we had enough to win this game. As each minute passed, void of even a whisper, the energy in the room began to increase. Each of my teammates began to gather strength from this masterful nontalk.

"As the officials entered the locker room to announce the second half, we stood up in unison and moved as a single unit onto the arena floor. Pat Riley never said a word at halftime. We played the third quarter like we were possessed. We clawed our way back into the game. That night, we were not to be denied. After our miraculous come-from-behind victory over the world champion Chicago Bulls, we all realized we were recipients of the greatest motivational speech that was *never* heard."

Sometimes silence is the greatest tool. Use it judiciously.

Parenting

A little over 21 years ago, I remember driving home with my wife and newborn daughter from the hospital. It seems like yesterday. Days before, I had purchased a new VCR. It came with an operating manual with diagrams and detailed instructions. The hospital gave no such manual for my infant daughter. Now what do I do? Two decades later she is a grown, independent woman away at college. Time flies. Trial and error helped us write the manual by ourselves.

Do you raise your children as you were raised? Or do you do the opposite? Or is it a compromise? What should your vision be for your kids when they finally move away from the nest and start their own life? Independent? Good character? Responsible? Solid values? All of these?

I believe the single most important thing we can give our children is the ability to make positive decisions based on carefully gathered information. People need to make solid decisions, especially in a crisis or moment of truth. They need to understand the dynamic of risk and reward. They need to know that the next move they make under those conditions and circumstances will alter the outcome of the event. And they need to make their choices with wisdom.

Will your children listen to their inner voice? It only speaks once. And it whispers. Will they dismiss it? Will they let reason take the reins? Will they not believe its all-knowing power? Do I get in that car? Do I go into that room? Do I walk down the alley? Do I say no?

Our children are only as good as what they think when we aren't there.

Sometimes we need to let them fail so that lessons can be learned, especially at an early age. Too many times we won't rock the boat because we don't want to upset, hurt, or even lose our "friend." Forget friends. We are the Parents. The Coach. The Guide.

Teach your children to think on their own. Let them fail (on the small, insignificant matters) if their decisions are wrong. And let them pay the consequences. Show them the power of the inner voice. Help them become decision makers of the highest order.

And when they drive home from the hospital with their spouse and newborn, they'll have a manual for raising their own.

Relationships

Remember when you first started dating your significant other? Just being around him or her made you feel giddy. You wanted nothing more than to spend time with this person. When you were apart, all you could think about was this person, and how lucky you were to have her or him in your life. When you and your significant other talked, the conversation was carefree. You talked about the future. You talked about your life together. And you talked about what you wanted for each other. At some point, your relationship started to develop a shared vision. Your relationship was no longer about you and me; it was about you, me, and us.

This was when 1 + 1 equaled 3 or more in your relationship. It's when you and your partner equaled more together than apart.

When 1 + 1 = 3, a couple is looking down the line: 5 years, 10 years, 20 years. The couple sees that they have the same shared vision. But time inevitably passes, and soon you're busy with your stuff, and your partner has his or her own obligations. Thoughts about your partner may still creep in, but they are not as vibrant and they're not as awesome, because other things have taken their place. Things have become complicated, and being in the relationship is just not as easy as it used to be. When you go to bed at night, you're thinking about your own vision, your individual goals. One person may even be going to bed thinking about another partner, not the one next to her. Pretty soon, you wake up and $1 + 1$ does not equal 3 anymore. Your vision is no longer shared. You don't talk about the future; instead, you're always talking about the past. And the only things you have in common are the kids and paying bills.

Is this where your relationship is? Is this where it is heading? Or is this where it has been? In a relationship, it's all about what you think.

Your relationship is only as strong as what your partner thinks when you're not there. Know your partner's goals. Know her individual vision. Really sit down and talk about the milestones that are coming up. What are the things you want to do? What places do you want to visit? How do you want to retire? What do you want your quality of life together to be?

Does $1 + 1 = 3$ in your relationship?

Work on your math. You'll have a better life and a better relationship.

Managers

With the average employee having 2,000 to 3,000 thoughts every day, one cannot expect the company to receive the full focus of all of them. Even during working hours, a team member's thoughts can change from family to friends to personal matters and back to business within a matter of seconds. However, a company can reasonably expect to get the most thoughts and the highest-quality thoughts from its employees during business hours.

Some workers think about business every waking moment of the day. They take their thoughts about business home with them. Others leave their business thoughts at the door as they exit the office. Every worker is different.

An owner, senior executive, or manager must realize that she does not manage people. She manages thoughts. And every thought translates into a literal action. When a person's thoughts change, their actions change. When actions change, the reaction is set in motion. Actions change, results change, and goals are reached or not reached.

Most senior management teams operate from a balance sheet or a profit-and-loss (P&L) statement. There are two types of P&L statements: a dead P&L, where you look at the numbers and deduce that they are too high or too low; and a living P&L, where you account for the thoughts that contribute to each line item. When management is looking at the line items for income and expenses to see if there is a profit or a loss, they are looking at a dead P&L. They are looking at it from a cold numbers point of view, analyzing it in terms of profit and loss. But when management is looking at each line item of income and expense, and recognizing the thoughts that contribute to that line item, they are looking at a living P&L statement.

For example, in a living P&L, the sales income of a particular product has to do with the thoughts of the sales personnel and the thoughts of the customer. These thoughts will formulate the sales income. Change the thoughts in that line item, and the numbers will change. Likewise, on the expense side of the P&L, if the thoughts of the suppliers who are contributing to that particular line item change, that number can increase or decrease. By understanding that there are thoughts that run into each line item, you can now begin to change those thoughts. This will start the chain reaction that will change the numbers in your company's P&L statement. But remember, the thoughts must change long before the numbers can change.

In the automobile sales industry, for example, a sales team may employ high-pressure selling—putting the squeeze on people as soon as they walk in the door. Sales will not increase until that sales process changes to make it a more friendly, comfortable, and relaxed environment, more conducive to purchasing a car. When a salesman realizes that he doesn't sell cars, but rather motivates people to improve their quality of transportation at a price they can afford, car sales will increase because his thoughts have changed.

In 1999, I began coaching Headquarter Toyota in Hia[ ]
Florida, a suburb of Miami. By 2005, the sales managers of the [ ]
pany doubled their personal income. Sales are at an all-time high. In
2004, they increased profit by 23 percent. Now the company is ranked
15th in the nation out of 3,000 Toyota dealers. This is due to changing
thoughts.

The next time you look at your P&L statement, look at it as a living
P&L. Look at it through a different pair of glasses. See the people and
the thoughts of the people that are flowing into these line items. Then
you can begin to make changes in people's thoughts, and watch the
numbers change for the better.

Get your P&L statement in the Zone, and you'll produce more
net profits.

Teams

Great teams have one thing in common. Every player shares the same
vision of team destiny. This vision is indelibly etched into the subconscious mind of each performer. The vision wakes them up in the
morning and puts them to bed at night. They know why they go to
practice and why they need to take care of themselves physically,
mentally, and technically. Each practice and game is one step closer
to the vision turning into reality.

In 1997, I coached nine players on the Cleveland Indians. From
spring training to the seventh game of the World Series, I observed the
common thread that connected each player.

In the clubhouse during all 162 regular-season games, you would
hear no gossip. There was no envy or jealousy. I witnessed no racism,
prejudice, or malice. There were no rumors or assumption thinking.
And I never heard one player second-guess management. In fact, I
never heard anyone discuss the opposition. It was as if the competition
did not exist.

What I did see and hear was 25 men preparing themselves physically, mentally, and technically to the best of their ability each and every day.

There was a discipline in the '97 Indians that was born from the self-discipline of each man. In a way, every player was selfish in his own preparation. They came to work at different times, dressed in different street clothes, and spoke with different accents. Yet their shared vision molded this motley crew into one force and one winning unit. Everyone on the team knew his role and respected the role of the others.

The team was committed to winning. Through discipline, they learned how to manufacture runs and how to stop runs from scoring. They collectively thought less than most teams. By eliminating all negatives, they could now just focus on executing basics within very simple tactics and strategies.

You could feel the energy once the game commenced. It was the fusion of 25 players and several coaches locked mentally in the moment. Each player was only concerned about the execution of the fundamentals of the game. And the sum total was greater than all of the parts. It was synergy at work. It was the Zone. The energy of 25 men were engaged in the moment. You could feel it. The crowd could feel it. And the opposition could feel it.

This Indians team had confidence. They not only believed in themselves individually, but they had an expectation that the others on the team would get the hit or make the play. Each man was cheered and encouraged by his teammates. When adversity would rear its ugly head, the collective force would not waiver. The players remained stoic in defeat and matter-of-fact when they won. And with each game, you could feel their belief and expectancy in each other improve.

Every great team has a nucleus of players that are the glue that binds it together. The Indians were no different. You could count on Matt Williams, Jack McDowell, Orel Hershiser, Jim Thome, Charles Nagy, David Justice, Sandy Alomar, Manny Ramirez, and Omar Vizquel to reach a high daily standard. You just knew it. They were prepared before every game. They made adjustments at the plate and on the mound during the game. And they evaluated their performance each night and moved on by burying the past, with only the lessons to be learned going forward into tomorrow.

The team was also rather loose. They were relaxed in every situation. And they exuded passion and enjoyment with every passing day. Yes, they were serious about their craft, but they still laughed every day. Twenty-five men could be seen playing a game they loved. You could feel the energy. And so could the competition.

There are many teams out of balance. The ones that are too disciplined become anal and rigid. They can choke under too much pressure. Some teams don't have the confidence. They lack the swagger that can overcome adversity. Some teams are too loose. This lack of discipline becomes their Achilles' heel.

It is this daily balance of self-discipline, concentration, optimism, relaxation, and enjoyment that fuses individual players into the wrecking-ball force of a great team. In 1997, the Cleveland Indians played baseball in the Zone. Their team formula can and will be replicated with the S.C.O.R.E. System.

Yes. Teams can get in the Zone.

Being a Kid

Why did you learn more from birth to five years of age than during the rest of your life combined? What prompted this super learning? My research from 1974 to 1979 with thousands of children from three to six years old revealed the following.

- Your imagination was at an all-time high. You acted the part of cowboys, Indians, princesses, and TV heroes.
- You never thought about the past unless an adult forced you: "I told you not to do that."

- You learned from the past through trial and error, but you didn't dwell on it.
- Your future thoughts were very short term: "We'll get an ice cream later."
- You normally went to bed happy and woke up happy.
- You had very little expectations placed on you. Mistakes were no big deal.
- You exercised free will every day.
- You trusted people without thinking about innuendos, rumor, gossip, and or assumptions.
- You were inquisitive without concern of embarrassment or shame: "Where do babies come from?" "Why is your skin different?"
- You did not worry.
- You lived the majority of your day in the *now*.
- You had confidence because you felt secure and protected.
- You could vent your displeasure openly: "Yuk! This tastes bad."
- You always expressed your negative feelings: "I don't like you."
- You didn't mind being alone.
- You took nothing for granted: "Are we still going to the park?" "Yes." Five minutes later: "Are we still going to the park?" "I said yes." Ten minutes later: "Are we still going to the park?" "Not if you keep bothering me." "OK, but are we still going?"
- You were a risk taker. Water . . . heights . . . speed . . . no problem!
- You could focus long periods of time on simple things like cartoons, watching an ant carry food, listening to the rain on your bedroom window.
- You played a lot every day.
- You exercised daily.
- You looked out for number one: "Those are my toys. Give them to me."

- You said what you felt and you were honest to a fault. "Mr. Johnson, why are you so fat?"
- You felt no racism or prejudice.
- When you played, you never thought about technique. You just played the game.
- You believed adults.
- Clocks and watches never mattered.
- The telephone was interesting but not really important.
- You had no bills.
- Your body was relaxed most of the time.
- You thought you could do anything. Everything was possible.
- You had deep sleeps. Alarm clocks were for adults.
- You could nap anywhere if needed: floors, backseats of cars, closets.
- You didn't like baths, but when you took them you made the most of it. How relaxing and fun! Showers were for adults in a hurry.
- You could always entertain yourself.
- Visualization was a major part of your life.
- Getting dirty was cool.
- Making mistakes never bothered you until the adults made a big deal out of them.
- Competition was natural, not something that was expected.
- You believed promises.
- You hugged a lot.
- You were always yourself unless you were acting out a fantasy.
- Who, what, where, when, how much, and why were your favorite words.
- You played a lot with your family.
- You saw life through different glasses.
- You noticed everything in a room.
- You loved the outdoors.

- You loved rolling down a hill, making a snow angel, going up the slide, singing loud, laughing, making milk mustaches, dressing up make-believe, birthdays, parades, puppies, seeing your cousins, learning to whistle, tricking your brother or sister.
- You genuinely loved yourself, family, and life.

Basically, you lived in or near the Zone. Isn't it time to be a kid again? I promised myself that when I departed this earth a kid would die in my old body.

Rekindle super learning. Increase your daily performances and remember this: good fortune favors the bold. Be a kid again!

Decision Makers

As a former professional tennis coach and player, I've had my share of controversy regarding line calls. One player thinks the ball is out and the other believes the ball is in. However, if you place a tennis ball just outside the end line or baseline, two separate pictures will appear depending on your viewpoint.

1. From inside the court looking out to the ball, you can clearly see the green out-of-bounds paint between the white line and the yellow ball. There is no doubt the ball is out. Period!
2. From outside the court area, the same ball appears to rest on the line or maybe just inside the line. You know it is in. You would pass a lie-detector test from this viewpoint.

Two viewpoints. Two opposite perspectives.

We have many disagreements and obstacles in life. These confrontations demand closure. In the past two weeks, I've assisted many people in making performance decisions. I've made some myself. Some of these decisions have involved more than one person's viewpoint. Some see the problem from outside the line, and some are viewing from the exact opposite.

In order to make the right choices in life, we must not only see things from another person's perspective, but we must also feel the emotion that person possesses. Mentally, we must walk in their shoes. Feel what they are feeling.

Before making decisions try the following: Like a judge in a courtroom, walk around the problem 360 degrees. Look through the eyes of all parties to the problem. Feel the emotion emanating from each viewpoint. Feel people's patience or impatience, trust or lack of trust, belief or disbelief, comfort, worry, and/or anxiety. Read their thoughts by observing their thought reactions. Listen to their words and observe how they are said. Absorb people's body language, tones, and inflections. Read their S.C.O.R.E. Levels. After all information is gathered, let your inner-body wisdom take over.

Sleep on the decision if at all possible. Ask for solutions to the problem while in a semidrowsy state. Most of the time, the solution will appear just as you awaken.

If sleeping on the problem is not an option, use your greatest gift. After weighing all the facts and role-playing the situation, listen to your sixth sense. It has an uncanny way of ascertaining information without your conscious knowledge. Mind your intuition.

Remember: great judges and great attorneys use these techniques. In fact, a great attorney could win the exact same case from either a prosecution or defense position.

More Resources from Jim Fannin

Jim Fannin has created several audio CDs on the S.C.O.R.E. System. They include *Life in the Zone, Golf in the Zone, Tennis in the Zone, Business in the Zone, Sports in the Zone* and *Baseball in the Zone*.

He has also developed an interactive subscription Web site (for a free tour go to www.zonecoach.com) where you'll find hundreds of audio, print, and video tools available for download to members.

Information about keynote speeches, seminars, workshops, and training programs for sports, business, or life is available on the Web site or upon request.

To receive a schedule of upcoming events or for purchasing his audio CDs or other information please call, write, or email:

Jim Fannin
P.O. Box 117
Hinsdale, IL 60522
877-210-2001
info@zonecoach.com
www.zonecoach.com

Index